The Daily Telegraph

CROSSWORD DIARY 2007

FRANCES LINCOLN LIMITED
PUBLISHERS

Frances Lincoln Ltd
4 Torriano Mews
Torriano Avenue
London NW5 2RZ
www.franceslincoln.com

The *Daily Telegraph* 2007 Crossword Diary

A catalogue record for this book is available from the British Library.

ISBN 10: 0-7112-2678-4
ISBN 13: 978-0-7112-2678-4
Printed and bound in China

First Frances Lincoln edition 2006

CALENDAR 2007

JANUARY

M	T	W	T	F	S	S
1	2	3	4	5	6	7
8	9	10	11	12	13	14
15	16	17	18	19	20	21
22	23	24	25	26	27	28
29	30	31				

FEBRUARY

M	T	W	T	F	S	S
			1	2	3	4
5	6	7	8	9	10	11
12	13	14	15	16	17	18
19	20	21	22	23	24	25
26	27	28				

MARCH

M	T	W	T	F	S	S
			1	2	3	4
5	6	7	8	9	10	11
12	13	14	15	16	17	18
19	20	21	22	23	24	25
26	27	28	29	30	31	

APRIL

M	T	W	T	F	S	S
						1
2	3	4	5	6	7	8
9	10	11	12	13	14	15
16	17	18	19	20	21	22
23	24	25	26	27	28	29
30						

MAY

M	T	W	T	F	S	S
	1	2	3	4	5	6
7	8	9	10	11	12	13
14	15	16	17	18	19	20
21	22	23	24	25	26	27
28	29	30	31			

JUNE

M	T	W	T	F	S	S
				1	2	3
4	5	6	7	8	9	10
11	12	13	14	15	16	17
18	19	20	21	22	23	24
25	26	27	28	29	30	

JULY

M	T	W	T	F	S	S
						1
2	3	4	5	6	7	8
9	10	11	12	13	14	15
16	17	18	19	20	21	22
23	24	25	26	27	28	29
30	31					

AUGUST

M	T	W	T	F	S	S
		1	2	3	4	5
6	7	8	9	10	11	12
13	14	15	16	17	18	19
20	21	22	23	24	25	26
27	28	29	30	31		

SEPTEMBER

M	T	W	T	F	S	S
					1	2
3	4	5	6	7	8	9
10	11	12	13	14	15	16
17	18	19	20	21	22	23
24	25	26	27	28	29	30

OCTOBER

M	T	W	T	F	S	S
1	2	3	4	5	6	7
8	9	10	11	12	13	14
15	16	17	18	19	20	21
22	23	24	25	26	27	28
29	30	31				

NOVEMBER

M	T	W	T	F	S	S
			1	2	3	4
5	6	7	8	9	10	11
12	13	14	15	16	17	18
19	20	21	22	23	24	25
26	27	28	29	30		

DECEMBER

M	T	W	T	F	S	S
					1	2
3	4	5	6	7	8	9
10	11	12	13	14	15	16
17	18	19	20	21	22	23
24	25	26	27	28	29	30
31						

CALENDAR 2008

JANUARY

M	T	W	T	F	S	S
	1	2	3	4	5	6
7	8	9	10	11	12	13
14	15	16	17	18	19	20
21	22	23	24	25	26	27
28	29	30	31			

FEBRUARY

M	T	W	T	F	S	S
				1	2	3
4	5	6	7	8	9	10
11	12	13	14	15	16	17
18	19	20	21	22	23	24
25	26	27	28	29		

MARCH

M	T	W	T	F	S	S
					1	2
3	4	5	6	7	8	9
10	11	12	13	14	15	16
17	18	19	20	21	22	23
24	25	26	27	28	29	30
31						

APRIL

M	T	W	T	F	S	S
	1	2	3	4	5	6
7	8	9	10	11	12	13
14	15	16	17	18	19	20
21	22	23	24	25	26	27
28	29	30				

MAY

M	T	W	T	F	S	S
			1	2	3	4
5	6	7	8	9	10	11
12	13	14	15	16	17	18
19	20	21	22	23	24	25
26	27	28	29	30	31	

JUNE

M	T	W	T	F	S	S
						1
2	3	4	5	6	7	8
9	10	11	12	13	14	15
16	17	18	19	20	21	22
23	24	25	26	27	28	29
30						

JULY

M	T	W	T	F	S	S
	1	2	3	4	5	6
7	8	9	10	11	12	13
14	15	16	17	18	19	20
21	22	23	24	25	26	27
28	29	30	31			

AUGUST

M	T	W	T	F	S	S
				1	2	3
4	5	6	7	8	9	10
11	12	13	14	15	16	17
18	19	20	21	22	23	24
25	26	27	28	29	30	31

SEPTEMBER

M	T	W	T	F	S	S
1	2	3	4	5	6	7
8	9	10	11	12	13	14
15	16	17	18	19	20	21
22	23	24	25	26	27	28
29	30					

OCTOBER

M	T	W	T	F	S	S
		1	2	3	4	5
6	7	8	9	10	11	12
13	14	15	16	17	18	19
20	21	22	23	24	25	26
27	28	29	30	31		

NOVEMBER

M	T	W	T	F	S	S
					1	2
3	4	5	6	7	8	9
10	11	12	13	14	15	16
17	18	19	20	21	22	23
24	25	26	27	28	29	30

DECEMBER

M	T	W	T	F	S	S
1	2	3	4	5	6	7
8	9	10	11	12	13	14
15	16	17	18	19	20	21
22	23	24	25	26	27	28
29	30	31				

INTRODUCTION

The Daily Telegraph crossword first appeared on 30 July 1925. The puzzles were supposed to be published for just six weeks, in deference to a passing American craze. The rest, as they say, is history. . . . In the intervening eighty-or-so years scarcely a weekday has passed without a *Daily Telegraph* crossword, and in that time it has matured from the simple crossword of 1925 to the current cryptic teaser which daily entertains and challenges a large chunk of the paper's readership.

The *Telegraph* has a core team of six compilers – one for each day of the week – with a couple of other occasional setters who also act as emergency stopgaps.

Peter Chamberlain compiles the Saturday prize crossword. He was born in Northamptonshire (where he still lives) in 1947 and as a boy he was fascinated by the black-and-white squares on the back page of *The Daily Telegraph* at home – nobody ever filled them in. Then, at the age of fourteen, while staying at a guesthouse in Blackpool, he found a completed *Telegraph* prize cryptic crossword in the lounge. Although he could see no correlation between the clues and the solutions, gradually he worked them out back from the answers published the following day – and a passion was born. In 1986, while still working as an accountant, he became an occasional compiler for *The Daily Telegraph*, taking over the Saturday slot in 1988.

The Monday puzzle – a favourite with many solvers – is created by Roger Squires, the most prolific creator of crossword clues in the country. He was born in 1932 and from the age of seven had always wanted 'to see the world'. Thus he joined the Royal Navy at fifteen and over the next fifteen years visited fifty countries. In bad weather, when based ashore, aircrew played cards for money but, as a Member of the Magic Circle, Roger was barred, so he began solving crosswords instead. At sea, without newspapers, he started compiling and his first puzzle appeared in the *Radio Times* in 1963. In 1978 he became the Guinness Book of Records' 'World's Most Prolific Compiler', a record he still holds, with over 65,000 published crosswords in 465 publications. He, like Peter, joined the *Telegraph* team in 1986 and has been delighting solvers ever since.

Ray Terrell, who supplies the Tuesday puzzle, is a relative newcomer to the team – his first puzzle appeared in the paper in May 2003 and he took over the regular Tuesday spot at the beginning of 2006. Born in 1956, he was educated at Pocklington School before attending York Art College, thereafter spending many years in a variety of jobs before moving to Paris, where he now lives with his partner and their son. When not chained to the computer, he teaches French journalists and broadcasters the finer points of the English language – which undoubtedly adds a certain *je ne sais quoi* to his puzzle output.

Wednesday's puzzles are the work of Ann Tait. A classicist, she taught Latin at a girls' grammar school in Gloucestershire before devoting herself to the arcane delights of crossword compiling. She also began her *Telegraph* crossword life in the 1980s – a decade when many of the paper's existing compilers ascended to the great library in the sky.

It is not often that there is a personal link between successive compilers, but Thursday's puzzle is created by a great friend of the previous Thursday man, Bert Danher, who died in 2002. The son of a veterinary surgeon and a doctor, Jeremy Mutch was born in Liverpool in 1947 and brought up on the Wirral where he still lives. Having left Manchester University in 1970 with a degree in Spanish and Portuguese, he spent many years in the tourism industry, and it was not until 1997 that he entered the world of crossword compiling, but his abilities have increased to such an extent that he is a worthy successor to his friend, Bert.

And so we come to the Friday puzzle – the hardest puzzle of the week. From the mid-1980s this was the province of Ruth Crisp, the doyenne of crossword compilers, whose clues were models of simplicity and elegance hiding a core that was fiendishly cryptic. She was well into her eighties before she decided to pack away the dictionary and retire. But who could possibly follow that act? Well, it obviously had to be a knight in shining armour, and so it was that Don Manley rode to the rescue in 2004. Born in 1945 in Cullompton, Devon, he was educated at Blundell's School and Bristol University and spent many years in publishing, finishing as a senior commissioning editor at Oxford University Press. He, too, had his first crossword puzzle printed in the *Radio Times* – in 1964, a year after Roger. But why the knight in shining armour? Well, if you see a crossword pseudonym that is a Don (Spanish nobleman or knight) – Pasquale, Giovanni, Bradman, Quixote, etc. – then you are looking at a Don Manley puzzle. He is a compiler for all the major British broadsheets (including those that are no longer broadsheets!) and is the author of the prestigious *Chambers Crossword Manual*.

The two occasional compilers are Ian Mawby, an ex-racing car driver, and Simon Martin, ex-RAF.

And I hope you will delight in the fruits of all their labours as you work your way through the 53 crosswords in this diary. Have a good year. . . .

Val Gilbert
Daily Telegraph
Crossword Editor

2007

JANUARY

1 MONDAY

New Year's Day
Holiday, UK, Republic of Ireland, Canada, USA, Australia and New Zealand

2 TUESDAY

Holiday, Scotland and New Zealand

3 WEDNESDAY

Full Moon

4 THURSDAY

5 FRIDAY

6 SATURDAY

Epiphany

7 SUNDAY

ACROSS

1 Anguish descriptive of Scrooge losing a pound (6)
4 They cut teeth (8)
9 Inform of tiny adjustment (6)
10 Proverbially remains cool, though often framed (8)
12 American tug? (4)
13 Become entangled with a writer of music (5)
14 Design a tailless aircraft (4)
17 You won't have a clear run in this (8,4)
20 Enters before the others and wins (5,2,5)
23 So backward about turning up for work (4)
24 What could be cuter or more seasonable? (5)
25 Endlessly scrutinise the horses (4)
28 Forces to enlist in the cavalry (8)
29 Cowboy developing a cough (6)
30 Unique description of The House of Commons? (8)
31 Tries to catch *Points of View* (6)

DOWN

1 Collector of items for a rainy day (5-3)
2 Anti-Mass movement? (8)
3 Craft lacking a prow? (4)
5 Educated at home? (5-7)
6 Chap paid at Peter's expense? (4)
7 Apply preservatives — a typical measure with new lamb (6)
8 Well before summer (6)
11 They prevent friction when put in a race (4-8)
15 Peer, but find nothing in store (5)
16 Mock taking in food (5)
18 Poor clot breaks the rules of etiquette (8)
19 Academic has rooms outside the university (8)
21 Support, but don't allow to proceed (4,2)
22 Compassionate chap put in the shade (6)
26 It's kept at one end of a field (4)
27 A drink all round when there's profit! (4)

NOTES

ACROSS

1 Everything in its right place (9)
9 Comfort (6)
10 Kind of paint not nameless (6)
11 Meant to be hit on the head but it's not well with its head off (4)
12 Summary (6)
13 Kind of government a Red doesn't approve of unless he is himself the governor (9)
15 Butter for the sheep? (3)
16 This kind of nap is not usually associated with blankets (6)
19 What these troubles in India are aimed against (3)
21 A locality in London created by the Adam brothers (7)
22 "Hi! Angus!" (anag.) (7)
24 Tree that is not prominent on the coast (3)
26 A five in the city is hollow (6)
29 Valuable kind of old china (3)
31 Feeling, and showing it, perhaps (9)
32 Many a bird is this before being roasted (6)
34 A colloquial walk (4)
35 Peter being urged to make an attempt suggests this room (6)
36 A measure, perhaps of its end (6)
37 Country of Asia (9)

DOWN

2 This able man may be the son of a peer (6)
3 This gun sounds rather doggy (6)
4 This man would be jollity itself if he had it in him (6)
5 A drug that has yet to be discovered (7)
6 British poet (9)
7 Character from *As You Like It* (6)
8 Natural "wireless" perhaps (9)
9 Title (3)
14 Plant often seen on a railway wagon (4)
17 Town of Spain (9)
18 "Tip a cheat" (anag.) (9)
19 Bone (3)
20 Bird (3)
23 Metal that becomes a disclaimer when reversed (4)
25 Gas that is certainly not scentless (7)
27 Unpleasant daughter of Eve (6)
28 Pleats can make fastening (6)
29 This bit of your car sounds rather feminine (6)
30 Where bunny is at home (6)
33 Colour (3)

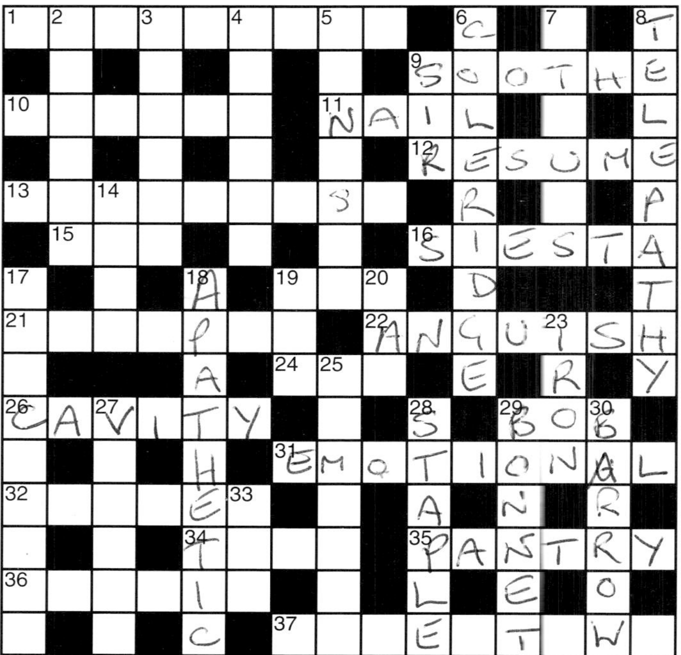

NOTES

JANUARY

MONDAY **8**

TUESDAY **9**

WEDNESDAY **10**

THURSDAY **11**

Last Quarter

FRIDAY **12**

SATURDAY **13**

SUNDAY **14**

Daily Telegraph crossword published in 1930.

JANUARY

15 MONDAY

Holiday, USA (Martin Luther King's birthday)

16 TUESDAY

17 WEDNESDAY

18 THURSDAY

19 FRIDAY

New Moon

20 SATURDAY

Islamic New Year (subject to sighting of the moon)

21 SUNDAY

ACROSS

7 Permission to proceed with eviction (9)
8 Include nobleman (5)
10 It's not safe to work on garden (6)
11 Table made from deciduous tree? (4-4)
12 Inclined to have catalogued (6)
14 Scold beater for moving (6)
16 Hand over free ticket (4)
17 Strut, being British champion (5)
18 Irish writer, we hear, is reckless (4)
19 Electrician leaves car behind square (6)
21 Unimportant person's criticism of thin wine? (6)
24 It's the state we're in, all the same (8)
26 In bed, unable to move (6)
27 Assumption one had contributed (5)
28 Vetoes about money-changing? Not at all (2,2,5)

DOWN

1 Grim line taken by common magistrate (5)
2 Pub profits from happy-hour sales? (8)
3 Mindlessly repeat the standard nonsense (6)
4 A detective force is sharp (4)
5 Monkey's bad mistake (6)
6 "Childish," social worker entered in dossier (9)
9 Bid for a stiff drink (6)
13 Hard rain mostly goes down here? (5)
15 Wet attempt at humour that fails to generate a spark? (4,5)
17 The boot for playin' in the street? (6)
18 One wiped out, totally defenceless (4,4)
20 Academic provides textbook (6)
22 Arrive in Cockney district from Cumbrian town (6)
23 The liquidity of French capital (5)
25 Toy you repeatedly break a bit off (2-2)

NOTES

ACROSS

1 Get rid of money that's source of rancour (7)
5 Look into abandoned chest for something to wear (7)
9 Went round and round to Delius' first (7)
10 Deduce nobody lacks substance in hell (7)
11 Game to resist — it offers no expressions (5-4)
12 Bounder executed animal (5)
13 Goes from container in case of threats (5)
15 It's hard to see through a pure pose when displayed (3-6)
17 Sea dog, for example, about to get explosive (9)
19 About to raise VAT — offer a counter argument (5)
22 A pound a minute for hard fought battle (5)
23 Newspapers, for example, enter into dubious act of appeasement (9)
25 Teaching instinct lacking at home (7)
26 Where football chants lead to row (7)
27 Ringed? Rung. Rang? No (7)
28 Allowed to take nine letters and got "Indulgent" (7)

DOWN

1 Where birds fight for room to manoeuvre (7)
2 Match brought forward (7)
3 Do nothing right — typical of him! (5)
4 Showing embarrassment at reprimand confers honour (3,6)
5 Rebuke concealed in church (5)
6 Feeling bad — not on the green for instance (3-6)
7 Difficult to start pushing this type of car (7)
8 One looks for a rubber (7)
14 If sitting, have a drink first (9)
16 Off to a dance with student — so the story goes (9)
17 The way pictures allow no time for surprise (7)
18 A lot of noise in support when ahead (7)
20 Troops ordered to take equipment inside (7)
21 Beat chap to the Circle Line (7)
23 Rumoured to look after set charges (5)
24 A stage in the kitchen (5)

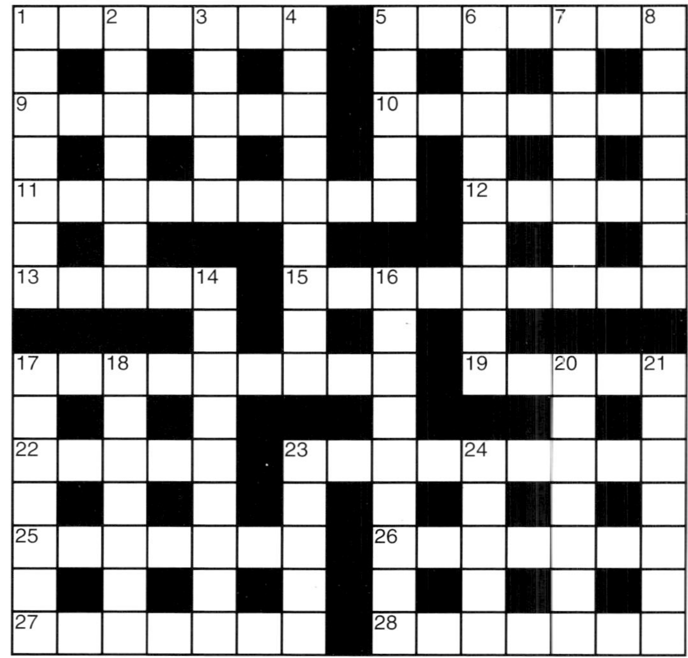

NOTES

JANUARY

MONDAY **22**

TUESDAY **23**

WEDNESDAY **24**

THURSDAY **25**

First Quarter

FRIDAY **26**

Holiday, Australia (Australia Day)

SATURDAY **27**

SUNDAY **28**

JANUARY & FEBRUARY

29 MONDAY

30 TUESDAY

31 WEDNESDAY

1 THURSDAY

2 FRIDAY

Full Moon

3 SATURDAY

4 SUNDAY

ACROSS

1 Thrive, shortening a wooden peg (5)
4 Churchwarden's fancy, a castle in Spain? (4,5)
9 Almost replete, several are admiring (7)
11 High post in aviation (7)
12 Cross back entrance (4)
13 Fighter aircraft at height of power (5)
14 Capital of retired soldier in artillery (4)
17 Her Majesty's fire precaution? (6-7)
19 Reviews Tate's peculiar mobile (13)
21 Trees shown in the Spanish manuscript (4)
22 Drops standards (5)
23 Vehicle parking? Complain! (4)
26 Worker returns holding Hindu garment for Russian empress (7)
27 A French flute arrangement that is easy on the ear (7)
28 Against dads reaching across to appetizer (9)
29 Vacation time for composer (5)

DOWN

1 Removes trees of deserts, possibly (9)
2 Moderately rich oil-producer on holiday (4-3)
3 Watch of king put on card game (4)
5 Feign unwillingness in impenetrable drama (4,4,2,3)
6 Some undervalued fuel (4)
7 Pop, say, with no head on it brings great joy (7)
8 A whisky to open holiday island? (5)
10 Special piano's brought out for this congregation (13)
15 Second follower of Robin Hood without a clue (5)
16 Char paper (5)
18 One goes up experimentally, using cricket-guide (4-5)
19 Scrap with man, perhaps, in breach (7)
20 Sad from tutor's first scolding (7)
21 Wide part of Essex, traditionally (5)
24 Walk with difficultly, one mile inside record (4)
25 Move slowly to small island (4)

NOTES

ACROSS

1 C/T (rather a disguised clue) (6)
4 These creatures are at home in two elements (8)
9 The opposite of true charity (6)
10 Often a host of men (8)
12 Oriental vehicle (5)
13 What bit of the track might be useful in the dining car? (9)
15 Gives an ugly sound in the SS (3)
16 Some modern "music" (5)
17 Nearly (3,3)
22 Describes one of the caskets in the *Merchant of Venice* (6)
24 A Dutch village (5)
27 Article always found in theatres (3)
28 If a woman has this pain it makes her a cheat (9)
31 You may say this word when you find it this (5)
32 Definite (8)
33 One of the FMS (6)
34 But not the great attraction in the aquarium (8)
35 The safest form of food? Not now, anyhow (6)

DOWN

1 Distinctly lethargic (8)
2 Spanish port (8)
3 The space isn't a square (9)
5 Wealth perhaps (5)
6 This commonly 5 brought to court (3,2)
7 Common dance in a foreign dance for an Indian state (6)
8 The saint who might make the war end (6)
11 Anyone is, in an RAF raid (6)
14 Revolutionary centre (3)
18 35 are not this fare (6)
19 Would a joint cooked in a submarine necessarily be this? (9)
20 The greedy boy's description of 35 across (8)
21 This sort of timber is no smaller if a bit is cut off one end (8)
23 This artist would be promoted on a division (3)
25 Paper with a leading article (6)
26 This is often kept in a case and a case is often heard in it (6)
29 27 if misplaced may be due to him (5)
30 Does this college date back to Roman times? (5)

NOTES

FEBRUARY

MONDAY **5**

TUESDAY **6**

Holiday, New Zealand (Waitangi Day)

WEDNESDAY **7**

THURSDAY **8**

FRIDAY **9**

SATURDAY **10**

Last Quarter

SUNDAY **11**

Daily Telegraph crossword published in 1943.

FEBRUARY

12 MONDAY

Holiday, USA (Lincoln's birthday)

13 TUESDAY

14 WEDNESDAY

St Valentine's Day

15 THURSDAY

16 FRIDAY

17 SATURDAY

New Moon

18 SUNDAY

Chinese New Year

ACROSS

1 Blast! All because of a pirate! (3-5)
5 The doctor's paper knife (6)
9 Does without nurse, but struggles (8)
10 Don't forget to pay another visit (6)
11 Left the country, but not by sea (8)
12 Writer for whom work's just a grind? (6)
14 Making over in a not over-way-out fashion (10)
18 Private communication of faith (10)
22 Minor villain going on foot (6)
23 A rousing militaristic call (8)
24 Rings right-minded painter on return (6)
25 Put the squeeze on alien holding British money (8)
26 Broke, so discourages (6)
27 Beast keeping catch dark (8)

DOWN

1 May be sore about short-weight slice given (6)
2 A service with some edge in the Netherlands (6)
3 Exercises inside but in full view (6)
4 Conclude cross is at risk (10)
6 Main race possibly in the USA (8)
7 Honour a simple man of the cloth (8)
8 Complaisant about party backing a hard worker (8)
13 Records the demolition of a Dorset town (10)
15 Case found by strike-breaker without key (8)
16 They pry with some hesitation into golf-club's set-up (8)
17 Abuse — when for example a sum is incorrect (8)
19 Stop engineers going over-seas (6)
20 Minor showing discourtesy (6)
21 Remove from the shade — let everyone enjoy it (6)

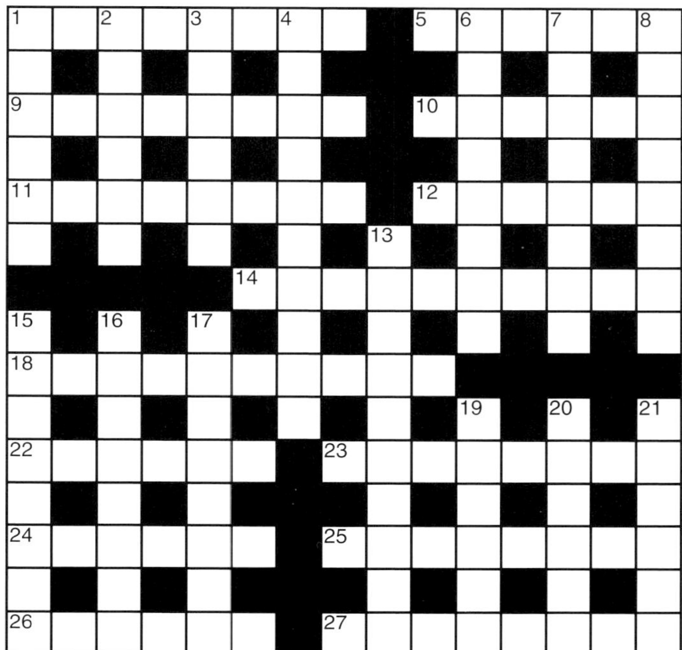

NOTES

ACROSS

1 & 9 Very easy to understand in the fortune-teller's sphere (2,5,2,7)
10 Measure of mercy (7)
11 Nothing included by confused nutter was false (3,4)
12 A kit's replaced in no end of panic for a cricketer perhaps (9)
14 Plant in a container accordingly (8)
15 He reverses better (6)
17 Melissa got up to the border town (7)
20 Serviceman (or servicewoman nowadays)? (6)
23 One doesn't care to lose it (8)
25 Informed in writing by this accountant (9)
26 Any chief involved in lawlessness? (7)
27 Woman boxer? (7)
28 Disconnect one from Paris with a jerk (7)
29 Dish from Mexico and Chile, a crumble (9)

DOWN

2 & 15 Very comfortable like a carpet-moth? (4,2,1,3,2,1,3)
3 Left cockney lady at northern town, or even more northerly one (7)
4 Opening for a photographer perhaps (8)
5 Namely nice switchback railway (6)
6 Onlooker, heartless boy, one on his feet (9)
7 Stiff and formal to be precise (7)
8 Trees recently stolen from military town (9)
13 Ran up with speed to provide a commentary (7)
15 See 2
16 Apply lotion when mob create havoc (9)
18 No credit given by place with money (4,4)
19 Diplomatic case? (7)
21 As an unbeliever, I fled in confusion (7)
22 Stabbed a rebel leader in haste (7)
24 She went round city limits with head tribesman for the tool (6)

1	2		3		4			5	■	6	■	7	■	8
■		■		■		■	■	9						
10							■		■		■		■	
■		■		■		■	■	11						
12							13		■		■		■	
■		■		■		■	14							
15				16		■		■	■		■		■	
	■	■	■	17					18		■	■	■	
	■	19	■		■	■		■	20		21		22	
23						24		■		■		■		■
	■		■		■	25								
26							■	■		■		■		■
	■		■		■		■	27						
28							■	■		■		■		■
	■		■		■	29								

NOTES

FEBRUARY

MONDAY **19**

Holiday, USA (Presidents' Day)

TUESDAY **20**

Shrove Tuesday

WEDNESDAY **21**

Ash Wednesday

THURSDAY **22**

FRIDAY **23**

SATURDAY **24**

First Quarter

SUNDAY **25**

FEBRUARY & MARCH

26 MONDAY

27 TUESDAY

28 WEDNESDAY

1 THURSDAY

St David's Day

2 FRIDAY

3 SATURDAY

Full Moon

4 SUNDAY

ACROSS

1 Vehicle that has been booked? (6,7)
10 Unheard and untested (7)
11 Job seeking (7)
12 Opening for a machine operator (4)
13 Start playing snooker, getting a series of points (5)
14 Dial out from Salvador (4)
17 Organ bright with flowers (7)
18 Many women have this combination of give and take (7)
19 Dependable way to limit bloodshed (7)
22 Cockney thief may end up in hot water (3-4)
24 The top copy required and ten more (4)
25 It's the minister's place to designate names (5)
26 Deliver without charge (4)
29 They're frozen in suspense (7)
30 Crafty ruse he'd introduced (7)
31 Host ministering to the needy (9,4)

DOWN

2 You can't get out if these are not kept open (7)
3 Bird is injected with thiamine (4)
4 They have got on in life (7)
5 One politician confronts every single charge (7)
6 It's unusual to retire in Tipperary (4)
7 Stalks out of the kitchen-garden (7)
8 What a person who intrudes in a row does? (4,4,3,2)
9 They are held up by the neck (6,2,5)
15 Maturing drink in silver container (5)
16 Go quietly to spill the beans (5)
20 A crime upsets a whole continent (7)
21 School principal to order a hearing-aid (7)
22 Capital cover for Roman soldiers (7)
23 It receives word of a murder plot (3-4)
27 East European not quite in bondage (4)
28 How about a call to slow down? (4)

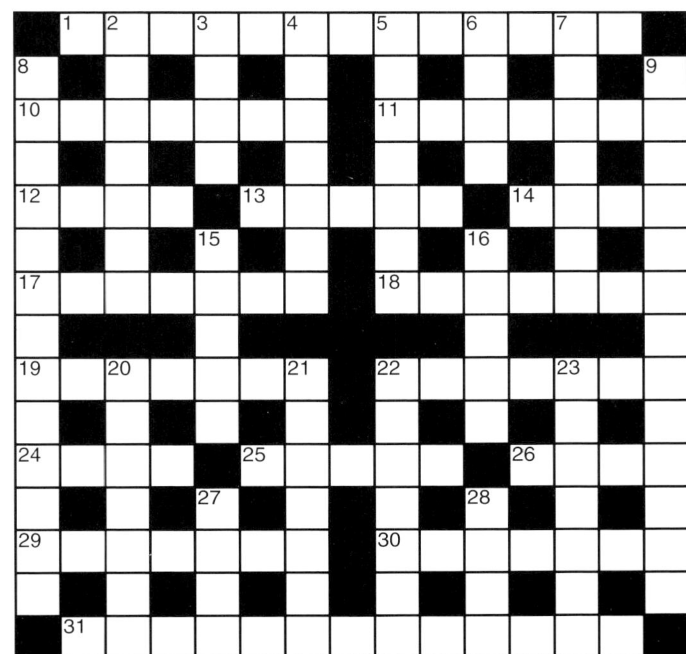

NOTES

ACROSS

1 Automaton is British in origin (5)
4 Find trash recycled directly (5-4)
9 Caresses and enfolds perhaps (7)
11 Frightened of small cut in wages (7)
12 Leave old Italian (4)
13 Cat flap close at hand (5)
14 Small daughter a nuisance in garden (4)
17 Tall, powerful, and very arrogant (4-3-6)
19 Men notice data are wrong — do a clean up (13)
21 Humble support (4)
22 Dependable, therefore top (5)
23 Proper margin put to page (4)
26 Improved? Somewhat improved, if I educated them (7)
27 Skill I found in man is out of this world (7)
28 Euphoric with heroin? On one's dignity, here (4,5)
29 Time for the opposition (5)

DOWN

1 Lawyer's fee for revision course (9)
2 Flags that are out for this singer? (7)
3 Have an impact, say (4)
5 Constitutional demand no monarch could satisfy (13)
6 Offensive vehicle may be fill of 24 (4)
7 3 took a bow, showing this skill (7)
8 Nymph is anti-liquor, notice (5)
10 Regular payment — one demanding a rise? (8,5)
15 Rival likely to flare when struck (5)
16 Take tea in multiple store (5)
18 You've half a chance of gambling profit here (4,5)
19 Stylish running? (7)
20 Transport company to publicise policy (7)
21 Tree at the seaside, say (5)
24 Angle of counter (4)
25 Available for nothing (4)

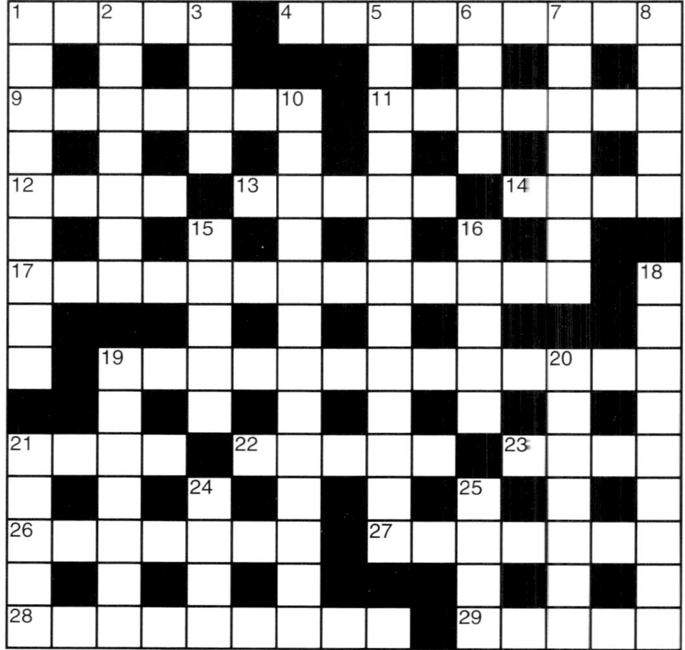

NOTES

MARCH

MONDAY **5**

TUESDAY **6**

WEDNESDAY **7**

THURSDAY **8**

FRIDAY **9**

SATURDAY **10**

SUNDAY **11**

MARCH

12 MONDAY

Commonwealth Day
Last Quarter

13 TUESDAY

14 WEDNESDAY

15 THURSDAY

16 FRIDAY

17 SATURDAY

18 SUNDAY

Mothering Sunday, UK

Daily Telegraph crossword published in 1965.

ACROSS

1 A seeming contradiction in terms of "down with payments and up with prices"? (4-8)
8 Rocket maybe designed not to hit the French island (7)
9 Opportunities for catches? (7)
12 A bank one could prove to have been organised by bandits! (4)
13 Slave to effect a saving (5)
14 Little beast a country evolves (4)
17 With sugary charm? (7)
18 Pulls or otherwise manipulates a carpet maybe (5,2)
19 A quack remedy from which most run! (7)
22 Settle on the spot for one's house perhaps (3,4)
24 Their enclave has a republic (4)
25 Arne's composition is a trap (5)
26 Before 12 the doctor concludes briefly what the gunners need (4)
29 The more changes, the more it looks like a maths proposition (7)
31 Right after the bowler's spell, yet late in coming (7)
32 "Take purse, Mrs!" (anag.) (12)

DOWN

1 Capt. Cook found the natives of Tonga far from this (7)
2 Check in the engineer first (4)
3 Highly suitable kind of office for a church dignitary (7)
4 Get back and put up the hood again? (7)
5 Top of every form! (4)
6 Watch from the yew-trees (3)
7 Many who fear it are relieved to discover there's a fine alternative (12)
10 For your enlightenment, there are 34 here (5)
11 He's a crack shot, and quick on the trigger too apparently (5,7)
15 6 fixedly? (5)
16 Maybe wields a bow with more than one string (5)
20 For those seeking suitably stout worsted twill doubtless serve! (5)
21 It's the least one can expect! (7)
22 Victorian venue for games (7)
23 Displays of old naval might, and the girl's up in arms! (7)
27 Did Sir Herbert grow in stature as an actor? (4)
28 Concede without stuffing (4)
30 Naval letters, but O, how correspondingly taxing they may be! (3)

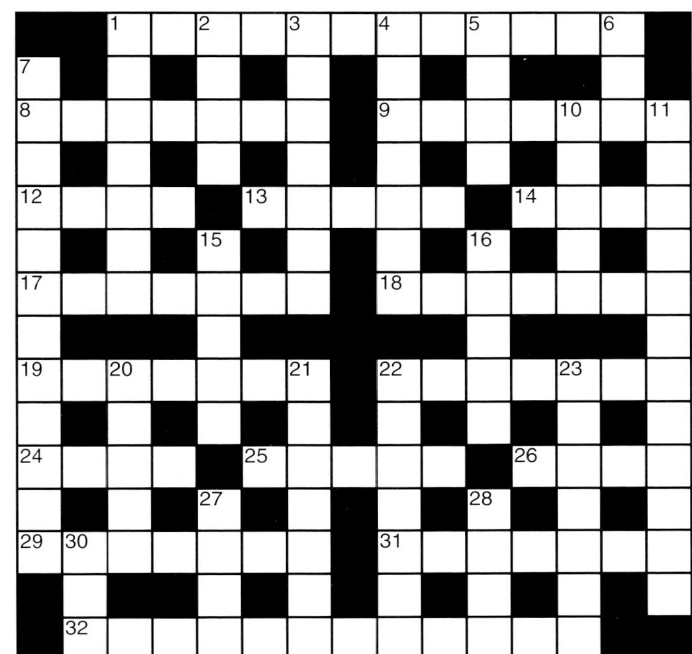

NOTES

ACROSS

1 Leads to complaint, when servants go on a bender (10,4)
9 A lot of brightly-coloured paper is needed (8)
10 Approach railwaymen's union (3-2)
12 The smart man takes his ale cold (4)
13 Hateful to bet a steed that's run off-course (10)
15 Trying to write a composition (8)
16 The right kind of floor for a long passage (6)
18 By word of mouth, or on a friend's say-so (6)
20 A broad view of Panama, or its interior (8)
23 A woman and man go together to the Spanish section of the church (4,6)
24 Shopping centre in smart London street (4)
26 Toy dog (5)
27 Distracted and confused when I enter football club (8)
28 In contrast to the Lorelei, these sirens are dangerous to ignore (7,7)

DOWN

2 To employ fewer is futile (7)
3 Sounds as if you, I and the French all used this sewing kit anyway (4)
4 In harmony about getting older together (8)
5 A car to avoid (6)
6 Japanese hand-cut meat might cause stomach ache! (6,4)
7 Given no blessing from the heart to elevate the spirt (7)
8 Splay out with leg speared horribly (6-5)
11 Steal pan and take chance there'll be something food in it? (4,3,4)
14 A normal, but not general, way to get a seat (2-8)
17 Unpunctuality makes a solicitor tense (8)
19 A town and/or a state with a king in southern Europe (7)
21 Fungus as life-threatening as a tiger, we hear (7)
22 Prohibit use of force if backed up within the island (6)
25 Film star reaches her peak at the side of her man (4)

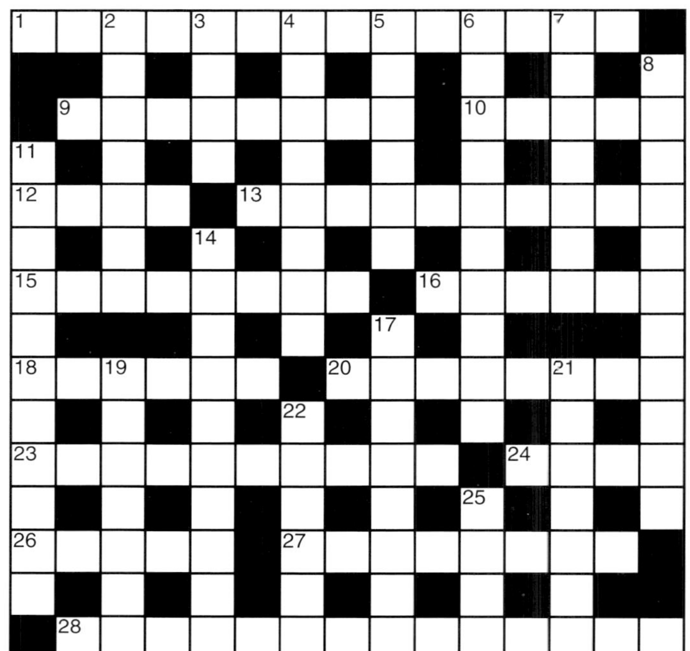

NOTES

MARCH

MONDAY **19**

St Patrick's Day
Holiday, Northern Ireland and Republic of Ireland
New Moon

TUESDAY **20**

WEDNESDAY **21**

Vernal Equinox

THURSDAY **22**

FRIDAY **23**

SATURDAY **24**

SUNDAY **25**

British Summertime begins
First Quarter

MARCH & APRIL

26 MONDAY

27 TUESDAY

28 WEDNESDAY

29 THURSDAY

30 FRIDAY

31 SATURDAY

1 SUNDAY

Palm Sunday

ACROSS

1 Fickle Lola married, with licence (7)
5 Programme charges (4)
9 Bedford-Paris is a trip for colourful fliers (5,2,8)
10 Regretted being impolite to listeners (4)
11 Smack — it makes sense (5)
12 Look for king visiting diocese (4)
15 Allure of a time zone (7)
16 With nothing showing on the dial (7)
17 Strengthening British leader, running in competition (7)
19 Hikes in the borders (7)
21 A little lower in the leg (4)
22 Key to secure large building of flats (5)
23 Raga playing here on Jumna river (4)
26 Volume turned up at home to impress visitors? (6-5,4)
27 Feel giddy in joy ride (4)
28 St Paul's under cover, lest pie is thrown? (7)

DOWN

1 A pound rate of exchange in Canada (7)
2 Exaggerated rainfall get her excited? (6,4,4)
3 The laundry used to be next to hospital (4)
4 Fainted away, being insolent (7)
5 Black endured being railed at (7)
6 Bassanio's choice of heavy metal (4)
7 Cheats relative of very soft leather (7)
8 Peg out to abandon Hamlet, say (4,2,3,5)
13 Wonder-worker in India hides a king in tree (5)
14 Stay pitched up? (5)
17 Wedding carriage unstylish in the air (7)
18 Edible jelly left in eating out (7)
19 Mum caber-tossing? How weird (7)
20 Fetter, Antarctic explorer who lost weight (7)
24 Board in castle (4)
25 Dwelling in heart of Yosemite (4)

NOTES

ACROSS

1 Deep colour (3-5)
5 Confronting a bad-tempered joiner (6)
9 A lad bore with disruption strongly like Joan Hunter Dunn (8)
10 Approached an artist — meant to obtain a picture (6)
12 Box Dickens' Sydney (6)
13 There's no call to stamp, the job's salaried! (4,4)
15 Army personnel hate delay (7)
16 Slight incline (4)
20 Sound features (4)
21 Greek administrator making no progress (7)
25 Got into a bed awkwardly (8)
26 Note left, always intelligent (6)
28 Assumption which is right about a man (6)
29 A metal found in fruit — metal of great value (8)
30 Less restrained, being a bit of a swine (6)
31 Duplicating expensive? Too bad! (4,4)

DOWN

1 Inspect damaged arches (6)
2 A table craftily positioned? (6)
3 A red nose might result, it's thought (8)
4 Girl back in the Welsh Valley she came from (4)
6 Virtuous, so has head start in class (6)
7 Love talks about Oriental functions (8)
8 Getting very heated in a wet sort of way (8)
11 Show larboard light (7)
14 Faced up-river and stood still (7)
17 Journalist giving heartless rogue a beer (8)
18 Squanders food (8)
19 He may well cut a fine figure (8)
22 Get through and support the engineer (6)
23 Venice is disintegrating, that's manifest (6)
24 Academic introduction for formal royal letters (6)
27 See possibly about fifty as different (4)

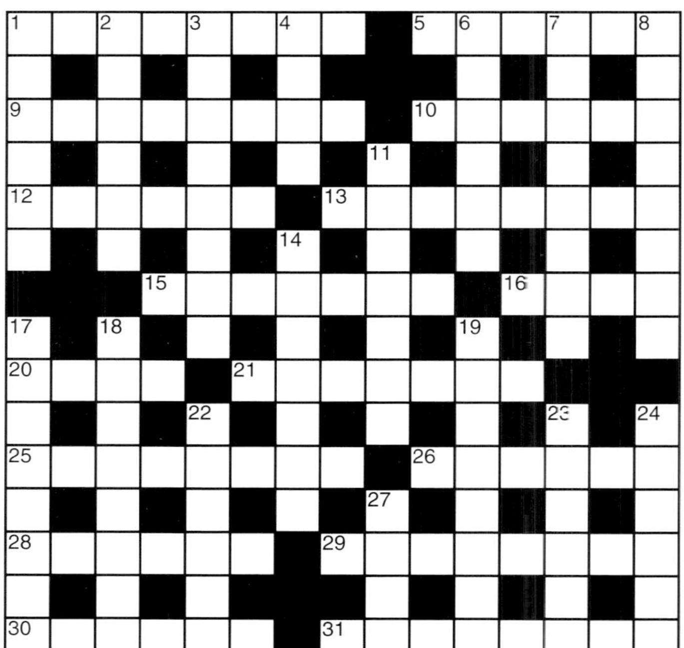

NOTES

APRIL

MONDAY **2**

Full Moon

TUESDAY **3**

Passover (Pesach), First Day

WEDNESDAY **4**

THURSDAY **5**

Maundy Thursday

FRIDAY **6**

Good Friday
Holiday, UK, Republic of Ireland, Canada, USA, Australia and New Zealand

SATURDAY **7**

SUNDAY **8**

Easter Sunday

APRIL

9 MONDAY

Easter Monday
Holiday, UK (exc. Scotland), Republic of Ireland, Canada, Australia and New Zealand
Passover (Pesach), Seventh Day

10 TUESDAY

Passover (Pesach), Eighth Day
Last Quarter

11 WEDNESDAY

12 THURSDAY

13 FRIDAY

14 SATURDAY

15 SUNDAY

ACROSS

1 Now Jude and little Catherine reportedly pass judgment (10)
6 Blackleg seen initially at advice centre (4)
9 Struggling foreign ref raised it to make a point (10)
10 A tune backing the song (4)
12 Do this at school and make sure you don't do it again! (5,1,6)
15 Many a flighty creature is cringing (6)
16 6 govern, not heartlessly, though full of hate (8)
18 Was on stage demanding much (8)
19 Evener distribution for a superficial coat (6)
21 Ignore move by an ineffective listener (4,1,4,3)
24 Knock member in bar on way back (4)
25 In charge of Caesar's doctrine about learning from experience (10)
26 It flies northeast after little hesitation (4)
27 Say too much, it's not true (10)

DOWN

1 Alfreda's colourless grass (4)
2 Right, not left, during month for panel (4)
3 Gear a skilled worker feels he is entitled to have (12)
4 Rumour from an eccentric going round (6)
5 Subjective? (8)
7 Given names, having wet the baby's head! (10)
8 Idea of naughty bairn facing heavy rain (10)
11 Capable of bouncing back better presumably (12)
13 Take all but the last bit on board, it's adequate (10)
14 Virginia in California on railway with fellow trooper (10)
17 Mingle in period nine (8)
20 Offering without hesitation to be some way away (6)
22 Girl in a poor way ails (4)
23 Duck trapped me in the corner (4)

NOTES

ACROSS

1 Conclusion reached after weeks of study? (3,2,4)
9 Put up in a row, as wolves are (6)
10 Meaty little bones going begging? (5,4)
11 Zealous artist coming back to make an impression (6)
12 Sends out a broadcast from St Martin's (9)
13 Woodland tree god coming under fire? (3-3)
17 She expects no aid initially (3)
19 Editorial about North British rowing club (7)
20 At length take a rest (3,4)
21 Pea soup seen at the zoo? (3)
23 Noel's favourite songs (6)
27 Stress the importance of a tube route, maybe (9)
28 Day-to-day volume of trade (6)
29 22 may, but the matador won't want to (4,1,4)
30 Part of San Francisco used by a native of 7 (6)
31 Rejects groups with crazy ideas (4,5)

DOWN

2 Table linen one gets through in New York (6)
3 Participating in a row or swallowing a gin cocktail (6)
4 Bits of coarse yarn that bring Kirriemuir to mind in the literary world (6)
5 Sort of apple Britons cut up in pieces (7)
6 Tall plants that need plenty of water (9)
7 Problem city whose footballers have thriven (9)
8 Can repent anew about being relevant (9)
14 What a firm may go on to when it is picketed? (9)
15 Regular supplier of milk that can't be criticised (6,3)
16 White flower that is highly sought after (9)
17 Are taken up for a time (3)
18 Drink enjoyed in a convivial environment (3)
22 What Peter ate with maple syrup? (7)
24 A setback in the building trade (6)
25 Set a record up for tableware (6)
26 A stranger to mint, possibly? (6)

NOTES

APRIL

MONDAY **16**

TUESDAY **17**

New Moon

WEDNESDAY **18**

THURSDAY **19**

FRIDAY **20**

SATURDAY **21**

Birthday of Queen Elizabeth II

SUNDAY **22**

Daily Telegraph crossword published in 1984.

WEEK 17 2007

APRIL

23 MONDAY

St George's Day

24 TUESDAY

First Quarter

25 WEDNESDAY

Holiday, Australia and New Zealand (Anzac Day)

26 THURSDAY

27 FRIDAY

28 SATURDAY

29 SUNDAY

ACROSS

1 Proud to make a fresh start at Rugby (4,3)
5 Forcibly puts forward awkward truths to school head (7)
9 Beer intended, we hear, to create disorder (7)
10 Having a baby, but not coming out with the truth? (5-2)
11 Brief error on the cricket field (5,4)
12 She goes round the Gold Coast (5)
13 The King has one of them (5)
15 Model paragon, he cares for waifs (9)
17 Hoist sail to break loose from personal unpleasantness (9)
19 Heather is a girl's name (5)
22 Spaniard, or anyone else with a present (5)
23 The grandeur of the Sergeant's Mess (9)
25 Flatter, most sincerely (7)
26 Choke — or throttle? (7)
27 Confined to college after a direction was denied (7)
28 Free news publication (7)

DOWN

1 Absolutely nothing on the radio — due to power cut? (4,3)
2 Lacking brothers and sisters, and just twelve months old (4,3)
3 Minister raised in the *Old Testament*? That's obvious (5)
4 With everything to throw around there's nothing left (5,4)
5 Switch lit up bulb (5)
6 Restore control to the country (9)
7 Soldier's stood up girl and married foreign woman (7)
8 Seeing about making it genuine (7)
14 Slow worker causing delay (9)
16 Weak team member transferred by coach, perhaps (9)
17 Pope with aspiration to become emperor (7)
18 It ends a flight in two ways (7)
20 State encouraging one to let the matter rest (7)
21 Harsh wind from South and East (7)
23 Consented to give up a vice (5)
24 Two learners in the mountains (5)

1		2		3		4	■	5		6		7		8
	■		■		■		■		■		■		■	
9							■	10						
	■		■		■		■		■		■		■	
11									■	12				
	■		■	■	■		■	■	■		■		■	
13				14	■	15		16						
■	■	■	■		■		■		■		■	■	■	■
17		18							■	19		20		21
	■		■		■	■	■		■	■	■		■	
22					■	23				24				
	■		■		■		■		■		■		■	
25							■	26						
	■		■		■		■		■		■		■	
27							■	28						

NOTES

ACROSS

1 Consuming about a stone, I'm guessing (10)
6 Check body of plant (4)
9 Added an edge in phone discussion (5)
10 Fletcher was a religious man (9)
12 Face unpleasant task, and grab the lead? (4 3 6)
14 Always, a saint is for good (8)
15 Pictures returned to the German dealer (6)
17 Trick silly parent (6)
19 Fully-grown deer worth a lot in America? (3 5)
21 Naturally they believe in selection (13)
24 Reckless man's appalling road speed (9)
25 Picture that's making cover of periodical (5)
26 After a minute, request cloak (4)
27 Two items for dinner table are in the window (5,5)

DOWN

1 One caught on the rebound? (4)
2 Skilful support or a number of commandments can be defenced (7)
3 Specially suited (4,2,7)
4 Understood vessel was reserved (8)
5 Railwaymen once came to Kent for tender (5)
7 Flirted? Sort of (7)
8 Tom remains puzzled by economic theory (10)
11 Quits knocking military drill (6-7)
13 Vote — allude to result with hesitation (10)
16 Indication by the way to finalise outgoing letters (8)
18 The curious toast is "Philosophers!" (7)
20 Accountant's relaxed with a type of ice-cream (7)
22 To summarise some final lines (2,3)
23 Hutton's means of focussing (4)

NOTES

APRIL & MAY

MONDAY **30**

TUESDAY **1**

WEDNESDAY **2**

Full Moon

THURSDAY **3**

FRIDAY **4**

SATURDAY **5**

SUNDAY **6**

MAY

7 MONDAY

Early May Bank Holiday, UK and Republic of Ireland

8 TUESDAY

9 WEDNESDAY

10 THURSDAY

Last Quarter

11 FRIDAY

12 SATURDAY

13 SUNDAY

Mother's Day, Canada, USA, Australia and New Zealand

Daily Telegraph crossword, published in 1932.

ACROSS

1 In this the last four are often reflected (6,5)
9 A ring for a game (5)
10 "Pater unto Ma" (anag.) (11)
11 An order of architecture (5)
12 One of 150 in the *Old Testament* (5)
15 Product of herds (5)
17 Bird (3)
18 Piece of wood that is unexpectedly not light (4)
19 Embrace (3)
21 Cold, but in China it helps to keep warm (5)
22 This Madagascan creature has swallowed 16 (5)
23 A clever little fish (3)
26 Divide this portion (4)
27 Flat bass (3)
28 Vessel sounds like a tool (5)
30 Kind of wheat; you must know how it is this before you can write it in (5)
33 You will find it in the tax (5)
35 Describes the space which you wish to fill (11)
36 Fish (5)
37 "Bring her one" (anag.) (7,4)

DOWN

2 A mixed shoot (5)
3 Distinctly important (5)
4 Fertile kind of 14 (4)
5 Fastener (5)
6 Fish for slang money (5)
7 Siege action — or is it a noble of the animal world? (11)
8 Herein might be found bears or bulls (5,6)
12 The kind of person who forgets to look before he leaps (11)
13 By this method of settlement one has right to part share (11)
14 Shape (5)
15 After needles this becomes in vain (3)
16 The bird 22 has swallowed (3)
20 Bright appearance (5)
24 Tree (3)
25 Mouth found only in Devon (3)
28 Town of Scotland (5)
29 Flower (5)
31 Out of this is not vertical (5)
32 "Whilst words of ——ed length and thund'ring sound amazed the gazing rustics rang'd around" (Goldsmith) (5)
34 Part of an onion (4)

NOTES

ACROSS

1 Nun's normal routine (5)
4 Theatrical troupe vacationing on desert island? (8)
10 Touching feelings, needing diplomacy on French island (7)
11 Melon makes Harry gassy (7)
12 Smaller amount to be debited (4)
13 Affirm the constitution (5)
14 Get through, or around (4)
17 Following trial proceedings (14)
19 Generally non-committal, but comes down hard on receiver of stolen goods (4,2,3,5)
22 & 23 Strings were pulled to get him on television (4,5)
24 Continent includes India, Siam and Vietnam (4)
27 I admit it, I sinned in Rome (7)
28 Completely full, having let to East End salesman (7)
29 The French CID is certain to be delayed outside (2,6)
30 Shabby sort of mat (5)

DOWN

1 What an accommodating chap! (8)
2 Gives support, but gets irritated reaction (5,2)
3 Stumble while hallucinating on LSD (4)
5 Nightly report is pure guesswork (1,4,2,3,4)
6 Angle at which to approach windmill (4)
7 Bird comes to moving end (7)
8 Pulls out American troops (5)
9 Emotional type keeps a record of his feelings (14)
15 You can have confidence in this financial arrangement (5)
16 A mistake to use this hook, we hear (5)
18 Adele enters piggery slowly, with dignity (8)
20 Encourages productive labour (7)
21 Developing ear, nose and throat scan (7)
22 Dismay fiend at Associated Press (5)
25 Get rail return to wild retreat (4)
26 Fight on foot? (4)

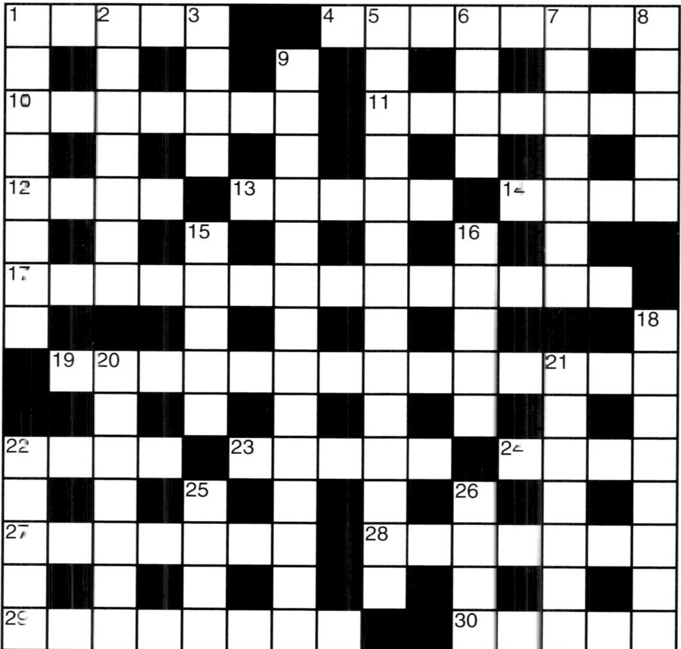

NOTES

MAY

MONDAY **14**

TUESDAY **15**

WEDNESDAY **16**

New Moon

THURSDAY **17**

Ascension Day

FRIDAY **18**

SATURDAY **19**

SUNDAY **20**

MAY

21 MONDAY

22 TUESDAY

23 WEDNESDAY

Jewish Feast of Weeks (Shavuot)
First Quarter

24 THURSDAY

25 FRIDAY

26 SATURDAY

27 SUNDAY

Whit Sunday (Pentecost)

ACROSS

1 Caribbean restriction on copper (5)
4 Cinemas do turn out such clowns (9)
9 Plain gold representation, still, on stage (7)
11 At university, made appointment to be fully briefed (7)
12 Behold commercial cargo (4)
13 Part of Florida hot, in a state (5)
14 I'll speak of Avalon or Skye (4)
17 Fresh pilot notices a nick (6,7)
19 In the wind, they blow over reeds (13)
21 Stopper for port (4)
22 Flat, open country (5)
23 Compete with women in examination (4)
26 She, for instance, in favour of sister carrying oxygen (7)
27 Bishop in petrol station finds rubbish (7)
28 Headless rodent will hold back the water in Holland (9)
29 Pigment employed in Kirkintilloch rectory (5)

DOWN

1 Prolonged episode of rigidity? Case aptly treated! (9)
2 One of the rabble put a shilling on final (7)
3 Those against one's development (4)
5 What, in gourmet recipe, is most appetizing? (5-8)
6 *Extinct Bird* Act II (4)
7 Mechanic can't begine to be biased (7)
8 Southern border of grass (5)
10 A French training programme of note proves wayward (13)
15 Fight mainly clean (5)
16 County flags (5)
18 Heels were repaired in another place (9)
19 Vehicle works with Masefield's lines (7)
20 Member of the Goosefoot family nips back to a club house (7)
21 Constable, artist and oil-producer (5)
24 Canon gives a hundred lines (4)
25 Archduke, we hear, is something of a patriot (4)

1 2 3 4 5 6 7 8 9 10 11 12 13 14 15 16 17 18 19 20 21 22 23 24 25 26 27 28 29

NOTES

ACROSS

1 The women should be given a hand when working (10)
9 Freshly-made drink (4)
10 He finishes having taken time in turning over duty-list (10)
11 Divulge hesitation about meat (6)
12 Stayed — and paid for it (7)
15 Stabilisers found on an ocean-going vessel (3-4)
16 College authority or benefactor (5)
17 Much regrets the ways of the French (4)
18 The right one will show dash (4)
19 Female with an over bright colouring (5)
21 This kitchen gadget rotates for mixing (7)
22 Small daughter is told to go, making protest (7)
24 A man, in preceding the Queen, must be near (6)
27 Malaise causing some resentment (3-7)
28 A point the editor made of necessity (4)
29 Transport for friendly force (5-5)

DOWN

2 Article on guys is the last word! (4)
3 Private doctor filling in this month (6)
4 Representation of nude man (anonymous) (7)
5 The first person to back up a Greek character (4)
6 Blunder into someone fastening up a dog (7)
7 Bring down the rate (10)
8 The youngster's grant's in a foreign currency (10)
12 Making little mark, so opting out (10)
13 Soldiers giving their names wrongly (3,7)
14 Many left town (5)
15 Report it's practical (5)
19 A deep creature's engagement token (7)
20 A pound in rises negotiated — or close (7)
23 Skinhead alert maybe but not so fresh (6)
25 A person giving voice in sepulchral tones (4)
26 Set against a diligent worker put over one (4)

NOTES

MAY & JUNE

MONDAY **28**

Spring Bank Holiday, UK
Holiday, USA (Memorial Day)

TUESDAY **29**

WEDNESDAY **30**

THURSDAY **31**

FRIDAY **1**

Full Moon

SATURDAY **2**

SUNDAY **3**

Trinity Sunday

WEEK 23 **2007**

JUNE

4 MONDAY

Holiday, Republic of Ireland
Holiday, New Zealand (The Queen's birthday)

5 TUESDAY

6 WEDNESDAY

7 THURSDAY

Corpus Christi

8 FRIDAY

Last Quarter

9 SATURDAY

The Queen's official birthday (subject to confirmation)

10 SUNDAY

Daily Telegraph crossword published in 1947.

ACROSS

1 His name on the screen is naturally a contribution to a good house (5,5)
6 This stood high in Egypt (4)
9 Two Scots reaching for the luncheon bill? (4-6)
10 A natural kind of covering to slip on (4)
13 Let this be a warning to you (3,4)
15 International agreement that takes in petrol at first (6)
16 When it comes to land work this certainly gets its teeth into it (6)
17 Its composition was associated with a lack of harmony (3,5,2,5)
18 Certainly not the result of turning a blind eye (6)
20 A sparkling match can this spectators' enthusiasm (6)
21 Able to prompt a heart bid (7)
22 Uniform with a nice balance (4)
25 Well-known means of eliminating opposition in fencing (4-6)
26 A familiar and capital spot to him who waits (4)
27 Could be a horny date, such as tomorrow will be (7,3)

DOWN

1 Animals moulded into parts... (4)
2 ...and one of them here is full of energy (4)
3 It has a caraway flavour (6)
4 "Atom plaint farce" (anag.) (yet power can be controlled by it) (3,2,10)
5 The pod one barely uses (6)
7 Burrow into nursery tales and you will find him (4,6)
8 Difficult to discipline, but led finally (4-6)
11 The diminished part is obvious, but it is really untouched (10)
12 You can say what you like, this is worth fighting for (4,6)
13 Staying power might be measured by the difficulty of this (7)
14 It is as colourful as, say, snipe around a marsh (7)
19 This can be applied to those not coming off 11 (6)
20 Enlighten unusually (6)
23 The man who has no ties probably shows it (4)
24 Vehicle three feet high (4)

1		2		3		4		5					

NOTES

ACROSS

1 12 inch elevation? (8)
5 Hothead travelled round south of the island (6)
9 Waste from a garden I removed (8)
10 Face, it shows how old Violet is! (6)
11 Beware of the view! (4,3)
12 Stuff two animals (7)
13 Now talented and of good appearance (11)
16 Thirteen leaves? (6,5)
21 Naval men in the grass remained still (7)
22 Advantage of a payment from the state (7)
23 Said it was very old initially and frozen (6)
24 Proverbially dead stud found on the way in? (8)
25 Worry about horse getting into the river (6)
26 Extremely distressed youth (8)

DOWN

1 Might it be played by a dishonest musician? (6)
2 Speaker in for a torrid time (6)
3 We hear it's a foul place to find egg producers! (7)
4 Dizzy blonde (5-6)
6 Docked locks? (7)
7 Getting up help with clan suffering bitter attack (8)
8 Senior eleven that's included are more sweaty (8)
12 Draught excluder on a building site? (6-5)
14 Lincoln met little resistance on river in south Wales (8)
15 Dodging the jumps (8)
17 Square fellow? (7)
18 No Northern Ireland man found it drip-dry (3-4)
19 A passion burning (6)
20 I'd lost out without being emotional (6)

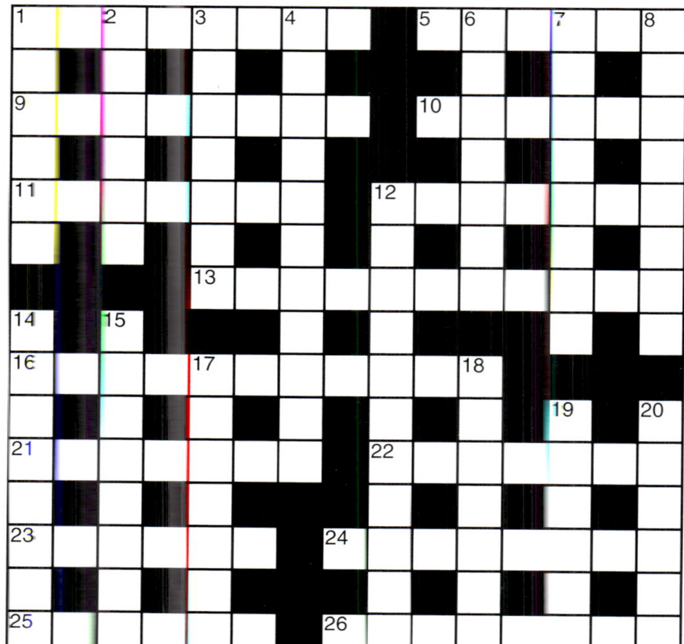

NOTES

JUNE

MONDAY **11**

Holiday, Australia (The Queen's birthday)

TUESDAY **12**

WEDNESDAY **13**

THURSDAY **14**

FRIDAY **15**

New Moon

SATURDAY **16**

SUNDAY **17**

Father's Day, UK, Canada and USA

WEEK 25 **2007**

JUNE

18 MONDAY

19 TUESDAY

20 WEDNESDAY

21 THURSDAY

Summer Solstice

22 FRIDAY

First Quarter

23 SATURDAY

24 SUNDAY

ACROSS

1 Finish — a sentence maybe (3,1,4,2)
9 Mark some golfer's cards (4)
10 Come in force, showing initiative (10)
11 About to take successful action to recover money (6)
12 Do such stairs make one gasp? (7)
15 Jury member has run-down, being swamped by evil (5,2)
16 Jar — in which to put coal (5)
17 Declines to see games of tennis (4)
18 Form of transport duty imposed on one (4)
19 Persuade an agency girl to start typing (5)
21 Noel's blazer (4-3)
22 Self — conscious about blemish, dark in colour (7)
24 It's erected for the reception (6)
27 Tariff or passage-money account? (4,2,4)
28 Reheated food in the mess (4)
29 It's diverting, though irrelevant (3,7)

DOWN

2 Is paid, we hear, for making large amounts of tea (4)
3 A lodge in state of disrepair and ancient (3-3)
4 Upsetting social habit often criticised (7)
5 I take friend out in vessel (4)
6 Girl in love we may daunt (7)
7 Relation supported by worker engaged in finance (10)
8 Inclination to break nipper's toy (10)
12 Why was I shy, awkward and irresolute? (5-5)
13 Her talents are involved with hives (6,4)
14 Composer, a Greek one, say (5)
15 Checks rising symptoms of measles (5)
19 Ring bell on counter where travellers have to pay (4-3)
20 Most woe-begotten pair (7)
23 One often out on the tiles (6)
25 Unusually cold part of the earth (4)
26 Metal press (4)

NOTES

ACROSS

1 Frolicking with South African clique? (8)
9 Life after death? (8)
10 Photograph without warning (4)
11 An overdrawn account (12)
13 It can make a man hate what is repellent to him (8)
15 They may be square or round? (6)
16 Advanced one good reason for sacrifice (4)
17 One French port is a key to the others (5)
18 Resistance units serving the Queen (4)
20 Teach fishes swimming (6)
21 Cleaning down (8)
23 Nonconformist who may be best in prayer? (12)
26 Well-produced paintings? (4)
27 Fish cooked as diners required (8)
28 The difference between imports and exports (5,3)

DOWN

2 Tell everyone girl's gained weight (8)
3 Great follower of Dickens (12)
4 Packed as a precaution? (2,4)
5 Going to drop one clanger (4)
6 Minimal sign of intelligence (8)
7 Thanks go to the team transport (4)
8 They often use clubs and bars, but should be fit (8)
12 Tender giver backing by Charles Dickens (3,5,4)
14 Competed a meal — while flying? (3,2)
16 Final appointment before military retirement? (4,4)
17 Two students put inside, paying for playground tyranny (8)
19 Unusual gloom in a remote part of Asia (8)
22 Some variation in game line-up (6)
24 Big lake rising in Southern Ireland (4)
25 Formerly in soccer style (4)

NOTES

JUNE & JULY

MONDAY **25**

TUESDAY **26**

WEDNESDAY **27**

THURSDAY **28**

FRIDAY **29**

SATURDAY **30**

Full Moon

SUNDAY **1**

Daily Telegraph crossword publishec in 2000.

WEEK 27 2007

JULY

2 MONDAY

Holiday, Canada (Canada Day)

3 TUESDAY

4 WEDNESDAY

Holiday, USA (Independence Day)

5 THURSDAY

6 FRIDAY

7 SATURDAY

Last Quarter

8 SUNDAY

ACROSS

1 Richard is shaky (5)
4 There and back, or circuitous journey? (5,4)
8 Come of age in US state prison (5)
9 Force very English virile types to church (9)
11 About to free king, using dagger (4)
12 Loud sound of bass — real agony (5)
13 Wearing boots, pressing hard into turf (4)
16 Betrothal gets broadcast on very loud tranny (6-7)
19 In which one crosses oneself, ready for yoga (5,8)
20 Modest opening — one club (4)
22 Latitude given to child for confused speech (5)
23 Dog may look as you talk (4)
26 Cheap tyre remoulded, a typical specimen (9)
27 From ruminant, rip edible part (5)
28 Carol hugs Erica, in case (9)
29 Visitor, the last to leave in gale (5)

DOWN

1 Challenged sin, being reckless (9)
2 Protection of original work, but imitation OK? (9)
3 American is a jerk (4)
4 Agitator who always returns to the same point? (13)
5 To be silent is stupid (4)
6 Managed to get central heating for farm (5)
7 False coin used to deceive (5)
10 Shrewdly practical, urge some solid protein (4-6,3)
14 Horrid type? Be a good chap! (5)
15 Object found in Inca village (5)
17 Fruit eaten, grin nastily (9)
18 Stand for show a second time (9)
20 Proposes to get funds (5)
21 Hiding place for money, say (5)
24 Defeat the finest (4)
25 Guns are raised to shoot this 14 (4)

1		2		3		4				5		6		7
8						9		10						
11					12						13			
				14						15				
		16										17		18
19														
20		21			22						23			
				24						25				
26										27				
28										29				

NOTES

ACROSS

1 One promised to have a note for finance (6)
4 Crafty stone-cutter (8)
10 Check power backup (9)
11 Lord North's warning ([illegible])
12 Disorganised but elegant crossing to a resort (7)
13 Run in to create terrible row (7)
14 Absolute quiet before poetic rendition ([illegible])
15 Abandon gold runner across the border (6)
18 Salesman's about to follow with hesitation ([illegible])
20 Gone to sear arranging food (5)
23 Disregard poor condition (7)
25 Money earned crossing a road is a loss ([illegible])
26 Negotiate a pleasant surprise (5)
27 Broadcast appropriate where aeroplanes suddenly lose height (3,[illegible])
28 Fun loving fellow in armed robbery ([illegible])
29 Courage at last in masculine, small-minded way (6)

DOWN

1 Government department concerned with pitch prediction (8)
2 Disturb volunteers in a French cottage ([illegible])
3 Food outlet's fear at ice breaking up (9)
5 Sad, forces threw out a piece of furniture (5,2,7)
6 One who fails to be taken in by close relative ([illegible])
7 Somehow ran into trouble and got the wind up (7)
8 Phoned up about the warden (6)
9 Care doctors lie about sorrow he doesn't feel (9,5)
16 Firm sleep or organization is one that goes to the wall ([illegible])
17 Record's attempt at hanging from the wall (6)
19 Intellectual approaches to education give good lead ([illegible])
21 Want nurse outside to ease off the pressure (7)
22 Case of sudden urge to tell all (6)
24 Defeated executed and devoured ([illegible])

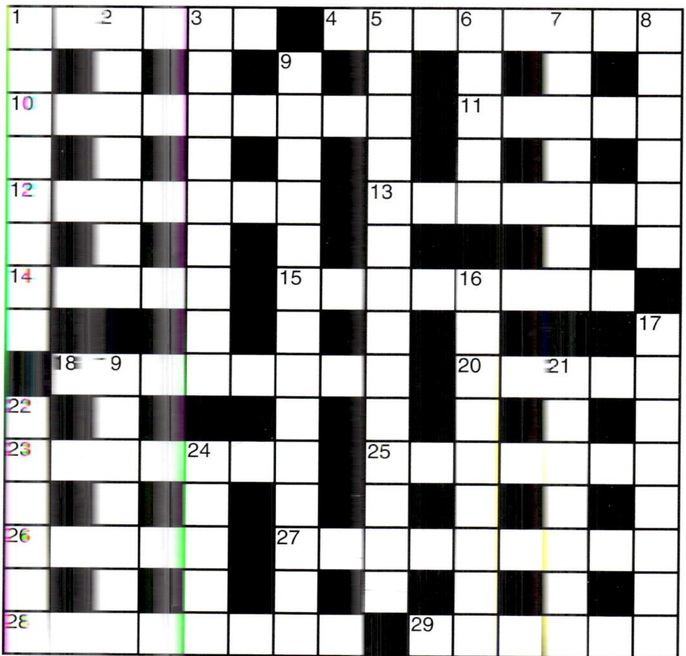

NOTES

JULY

MONDAY **9**

TUESDAY **10**

WEDNESDAY **11**

THURSDAY **12**

Holiday, Northern Ireland (Battle of the Boyne)

FRIDAY **13**

SATURDAY **14**

New Moon

SUNDAY **15**

St Swithin's Day

WEEK 29 **2007**

JULY

16 MONDAY

17 TUESDAY

18 WEDNESDAY

19 THURSDAY

20 FRIDAY

21 SATURDAY

22 SUNDAY

First Quarter

ACROSS

1 Avoid remote stronghold (4,3,2,3,3)
9 Fancy puzzling? (9)
10 Ear is injured in lift (5)
11 Once away, for this reason (5)
12 Divested, couldn't he go out (9)
13 Assassin said to be a winter-sports enthusiast (8)
14 Second owner of useful cat (6)
16 Heart-warming bivalve mollusc? (6)
18 It's troublesome in hollows for these bridge-builders (8)
22 Path indicates groups of travelling entertainers (4,5)
23 Novel girl embraces one in a lofty place (5)
24 Daggers drawn? (5)
25 Old instrument of one advanced in red wine (9)
26 Junior travellers putting up with Holst, the elusory arranger (5,10)

DOWN

1 Champions sometimes taken on board (7)
2 Understanding French? (7)
3 Whirling dervish lit gloom of Anglo-Irish playwright (6,9)
4 He denigrates what he tracks down about the Dutch (8)
5 Mostly modern company shows durable wall-painting (6)
6 Distress raised in place of school (6,2,3,4)
7 Contorts in pain from legal document he's received (7)
8 One giving up ride in Ely, possibly (7)
15 Cardinal alarm a songbird? (8)
16 Running quickly over nursery-rhyme (7)
17 French cat on water in bottling-premises? (7)
19 Jabber in the clinic? (7)
20 Hustles awkwardly in gumshoes (7)
21 No chop, minced, goes over Mexican dressing (6)

NOTES

ACROSS

1 Instant turn-back (5,6)
9 Spreading on treacle allowed variation (9)
10 Ruthless one certainly was not! (5)
11 Charges as the afternoon begins (6)
12 Disparages article by new press editor ([illegible])
13 A member of the family in hospital? (6)
15 Maybe a [illegible] used influence (8)
18 Left, and that's ominous! (8)
19 Delay retirement (4,[illegible])
21 Wear — a piece of underwear — is put backwards (8)
23 Novel trade (6)
26 Exemplary, though singular business arrangement ([illegible])
27 A record of ups and downs in the main ([illegible]-5)
28 Bard [illegible] showing age (11)

DOWN

1 Governors formerly appearing a bit reflective on board (7)
2 A city story about the fifties (5)
3 The fatigue of residents after moving ([illegible])
4 A bird in danger — nearly extinct (4)
5 Viewed too much, so must be supervised (8)
6 Man writing poetry finished about noon (5)
7 Many [illegible] over the French contract ([illegible])
8 Ever [illegible] scent — not freely available ([illegible])
14 Sol[illegible] various odd items (8)
16 Consumers may well get all wound up (9)
17 "Disgusted" was up in arms (8)
18 Making great efforts to get pounds in discount (7)
20 The lazy will see newsmen around mid-week (7)
22 Being confused, loves to find an answer (5)
24 Country maybe as currency no longer (5)
25 Engineers set up running water in Germany ([illegible])

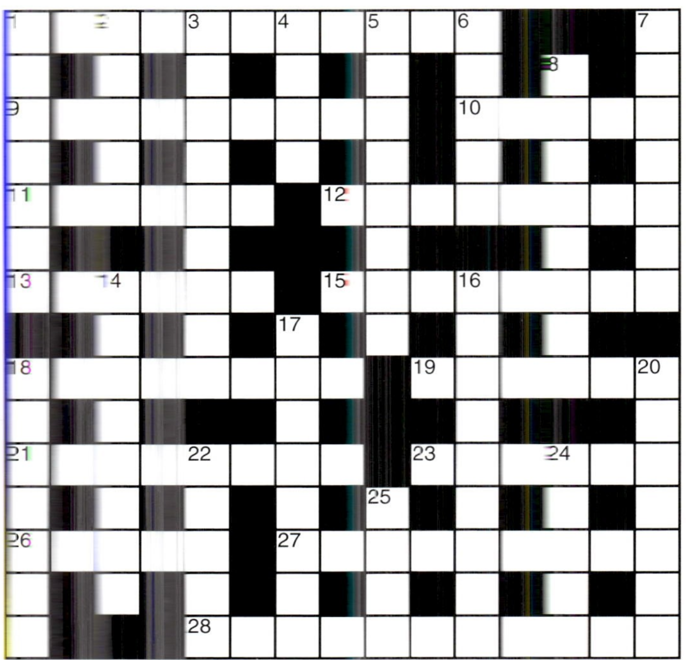

NOTES

JULY

MONDAY **23**

TUESDAY **24**

WEDNESDAY **25**

THURSDAY **26**

FRIDAY **27**

SATURDAY **28**

SUNDAY **29**

JULY & AUGUST

30 MONDAY

Full Moon

31 TUESDAY

1 WEDNESDAY

2 THURSDAY

3 FRIDAY

4 SATURDAY

5 SUNDAY

Last Quarter

ACROSS

1 Recover small open truck (4-2)
4 State one getting in the loot was a rascal (8)
10 One palls, content to be in the country (5)
11 I repeatedly name footballer who's a manager (9)
12 In luck having sails and tackle on the ship (7)
13 Had put one's foot it in? (7)
14 All events of course are listed in it (6,8)
17 MPs' do (9,5)
21 A redhead's remarkably nice with the poison! (7)
23 One who won't be found out? (7)
24 Reversal of policy concerning nervous shock (5-4)
25 One leaving hostilities in Greek capital during the squeeze (5)
26 Cure for lovesickness? (8)
27 State raw material has almost disappeared (6)

DOWN

1 Peg previously had protective cover (8)
2 200 in island I love produced free musical composition (9)
3 Forget a French king who preceded Napoleon initially (7)
5 Studies made by William at ten on northern and southern heavenly groups (14)
6 Have a rest at length (3,4)
7 During midweek I gently cleaned (5)
8 Go near troublesome place in Spain (6)
9 Order at Wimbledon or in hall of justice perhaps (7,2,5)
15 Reducing a loan (9)
16 The very lightest thing could upset dog with Henry (8)
18 I'd get in struggling, having made light of it! (7)
19 Pile on raw material during peacetime (7)
20 Parents going round an American country (6)
22 Sunday left for recreation (5)

NOTES

ACROSS

6 With which one suffers a lack of balance (3-,9)

8 Some card-games supplied by a stationer (5)

9 A ticket and a drink is what a traveller may need (8)

10 Girl Friday, no cook (3)

11 Way change of date may be expressed (6)

12 Note strange sort of desperado (6)

14 He takes obstacles in his stride (7)

16 Gather that the boxer is slightly in the lead? (5,2)

20 Skilfully holding back confusion in meeting (8)

23 Tone taken by doctor in fatigue (6)

24 For the returning traveller (3)

25 Class of good scholars (8)

26 Arch no different from others (6)

27 Unimportant Arab chiefs, we hear (2,5,6)

DOWN

1 Girl restrained but persistent (8)

2 Breakfast or lord? (8)

3 Discharge notice on attendant (7)

4 Here indeed is one man of genius (6)

5 Pitch letter on American college grounds (6)

6 Yet it might incur a sharp answer (5,8)

7 New players in the Rugby team (5,8)

13 Animal found in decreasing numbers (3)

15 Hit fly before lunch (3)

17 Completely wrong, overcorrect (6)

18 Aims keen to gain a similar title (8)

19 The work is somewhat mechanical, but character-forming (7)

21 Green party finally contrived to get power (6)

22 Incorrect to be said to be prejudiced (6)

NOTES

AUGUST

MONDAY **6**

Summer Bank Holiday, Scotland and Republic of Ireland

TUESDAY **7**

WEDNESDAY **8**

THURSDAY **9**

FRIDAY **10**

SATURDAY **11**

SUNDAY **12**

New Moon

WEEK 33 2007

AUGUST

13 MONDAY

14 TUESDAY

15 WEDNESDAY

16 THURSDAY

17 FRIDAY

18 SATURDAY

19 SUNDAY

Daily Telegraph crossword published in 1938.

ACROSS

1 Because of which criminals are nearly all hand in glove (12)
8 An unkind blow (3,4)
9 Put in a plant, as estimated (7)
11 A Hindoo god might provide his rank (7)
12 AD is half expanded in this river (7)
13 With the heart doubled it might bathe in itself (5)
14 Uncomfortable (3,2,4)
16 This provides a fair opportunity for giddy goings-on (9)
19 Unkind cuts (5)
21 Idea originated by a second person (7)
23 This part of London is forbidden to the motorist at midnight (7)
24 Piece of English legislature that was made possible by South American diplomacy (4,3)
25 No, a bad egg would not be appropriate at this meal (4,3)
26 You could bet your bottom dollar on this race — it would be disposing of silver anyway (7,5)

DOWN

1 The barometer may be this, but it's the weather that will break (7)
2 This rules out the brace (7)
3 Green and I become a listener in the finish (9)
4 The source of Helen's frocks? (5)
5 Sow (7)
6 A mythical queen (7)
7 This drink would not hurt a baby (4,3,5)
10 Red? (6,6)
15 It carries no cargo, but that doers not account for its name (9)
17 A useful mineral (4,3)
18 J class yachts would hardly use this bit of canvas (7)
19 One of the USA (7)
20 China, being this, may be easily partitioned (7)
22 Large part of 6 (5)

NOTES

ACROSS

1 American politician (9)
9 That's enough! — dreadful moron gets the point (2,4)
10 Excellent conifer, condition about right (5-4)
11 Detail person in debt (6)
12 Alsatian's role in *Dads' Army*? (4,5)
13 He'll trim Figaro's role (6)
17 Top hat (3)
19 An honour for the very finest nightspot? (3,5,2,5)
20 Joke gets silence (3)
21 Plea about victory in Europe from women Germans executed (6)
25 Put right in the head (9)
26 Position giving back-up to nobleman (6,3)
27 Area of grammar gives mishaps in pronunciation (9)
28 Boarder that pays deposit (6)
29 Jenny likes tell a good story (4, [illegible])

DOWN

2 Instrument stand — carelessly dropped (6)
3 One checking bed canopy (6)
4 Start to grow vegetable (6)
5 Bad weather in China? That's not so important (1,5,2,1,3)
6 Play patience (9)
7 Colour that may give boy allure (5,4)
8 Ambassador with speech revealing high-level cover-up (9)
14 Reserve store of pickles to cook (9)
15 Not a condition one would freely accept (9)
16 Passed exam, with reservation (9)
17 Stocking filler? (3)
18 Maybe a racing animal to follow (3)
22 Still one doesn't exhibit this proposal (6)
23 Better wear for good clothes (6)
24 Sportsman's run under barrier (6)

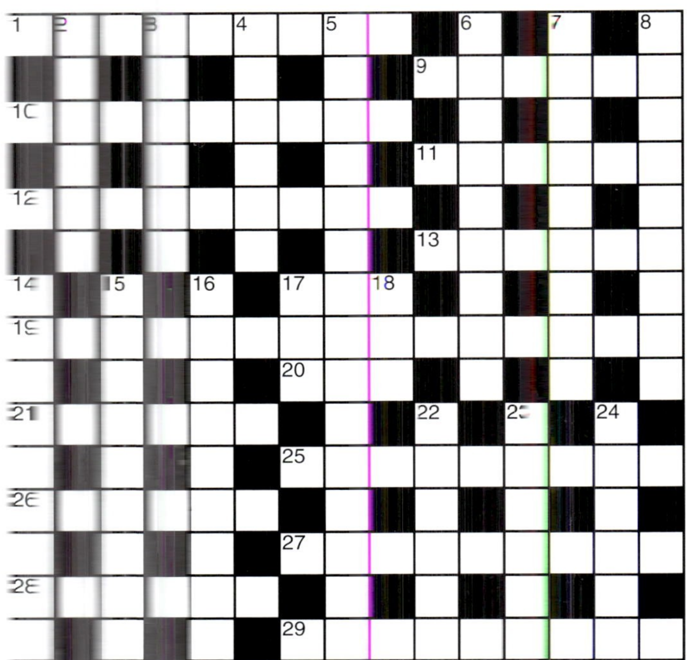

NOTES

AUGUST

MONDAY **20**

First Quarter

TUESDAY **21**

WEDNESDAY **22**

THURSDAY **23**

FRIDAY **24**

SATURDAY **25**

SUNDAY **26**

AUGUST & SEPTEMBER

27 MONDAY

Summer Bank Holiday, UK (exc. Scotland)

28 TUESDAY

Full Moon

29 WEDNESDAY

30 THURSDAY

31 FRIDAY

1 SATURDAY

2 SUNDAY

Father's Day, Australia and New Zealand

ACROSS

1 Crazy cricketers (4)
3 Signal from union leader in church (3)
5 Cut off caller with psychological kink (4-2)
8 Heavenly home, but there's a small drawback (6)
9 Co-operate in drama-dance production (4,4)
10 The gunman will shoot, despite dire punishment (4-4)
11 Son accompanies enchanting lady, for a change (6)
12 A dictionary used by barristers (8)
13 Can the Bavarian light fires with it? (6)
15 Sailors tucked into meat in spring (6)
18 They turn out English champions (8)
20 Kitty Fisher found what she lost — a piece of jewellery (6)
21 Fantasising whilst making marinade (2,1,5)
23 Reaching position of authority (2,6)
24 One fellow and no more? Would it were so! (2,4)
25 Protective covering one needs to step around (3-3)
26 Longing for some witty entertainment (3)
27 Hurries back from brief trip (4)

DOWN

1 Brazen redhead in the party (5)
2 The groom is a steady chap (9)
3 Course assistant occupied by many a coarse yarn (7)
4 Fast-talking ensures speedy GPO service (7,8)
5 Boss determined to display audio receiver (7)
6 Acknowledged that George initially pontificated (7)
7 Fish and veg served in lager (9)
12 Obliging inclination to offer royal annuities (5,4)
14 No riotous assembly is disreputable (9)
16 About to ride a bike to aid conservation (7)
17 Intimate enabled medic to get work (3,4)
19 Hindu queen embraced by Scotsman from the Middle East (7)
22 Could possibly meet an American Indian (5)

1			2	■	3		4	■	5			6		7
	■	■		■		■		■		■	■		■	
8						■	9							
	■	■		■		■		■		■	■		■	
10								■	11					
■	■	■		■		■		■		■	■		■	
12								■	13		14			
	■	■		■	■	■		■	■	■		■	■	
15		16			17	■	18		19					
	■		■	■		■		■		■		■	■	■
20						■	21							22
	■		■	■		■		■		■		■	■	
23								■	24					
	■		■	■		■		■		■		■	■	
25						■	26			■	27			

NOTES

ACROSS

1 Go along with Bill joining band (9)
8 Fancy cushions pad it in curator's office (13)
11 Like tough grass — but thin (5)
12 Swift brute showing return of dried grass-circles (5)
13 Whine from stable attendant (5)
16 After work, I took meal — it makes one drowsy (6)
17 Swear falsely about name in defence (6)
18 Wild party at fifty for this composer? (5)
19 General method of play (6)
20 Light first let in, perhaps, as beam over door (6)
21 Desire youth leader to be stripping? (6)
24 Body of scouts given rotten time on the way back (5)
26 Fly from a ship in trouble (5)
27 What may be revealed in ancient tombs, or, time-capsule broken open? (3,5)
28 Dealer does business with people (9)

DOWN

2 Tobacco pipes short in Scotland (5)
3 Testing time in gold trade (6)
4 Transfusion fluid from Malpas (6)
5 Unpleasant street in any form? (5)
6 Kids are brought up in one (8,5)
7 Get hanging in there as fight fails? (13)
9 Leaflets about rare minor bums (9)
10 Pinched-looking old timer? (4-5)
13 A green girl often (5)
14 Eastern girls all together in parts of roofs (5)
15 Match fit (5)
22 Champion at university, to endure (6)
23 She sits nervously in paper for diploma? (6)
25 Horse with heart? (5)
26 A near-collapse in battle area (5)

NOTES

SEPTEMBER

MONDAY **3**

Holiday, Canada (Labour Day) and USA (Labor Day)

TUESDAY **4**

Last Quarter

WEDNESDAY **5**

THURSDAY **6**

FRIDAY **7**

SATURDAY **8**

SUNDAY **9**

2007

SEPTEMBER

10 MONDAY

11 TUESDAY

New Moon

12 WEDNESDAY

13 THURSDAY

Jewish New Year (Rosh Hashanah)
First Day of Ramadân (subject to sighting of the moon)

14 FRIDAY

15 SATURDAY

16 SUNDAY

ACROSS

1 People offering professional models (9)
9 A near thing for the cameraman! (5-2)
10 Tough guy hits back with lash (7)
11 Put inside a letter and then seal (7)
12 Set off, and please walk (9)
14 In consequence some paper investigated (8)
15 Return to original owners about the green (6)
17 They stick up for those wanting to get a look-in (7)
20 More mysterious always, and that is right (6)
23 Left before about one in the doorway (8)
25 Fraternal member, though not even a peer (3,6)
26 So-called lion-man running wild (7)
27 Try to accept the growth of moorland (7)
28 Record is turning, left on by a Greek character (7)
29 Lavish with one's drink in time (9)

DOWN

2 Tripe so prepared is making a comeback (7)
3 He's made a promise — a part in the exercises (7)
4 Nathaniel in step? Rot! (8)
5 Shade required for some projected entertainment (6)
6 The company not in favour of proceeding (9)
7 Bird sanctuary organised by a woman on certain lines (7)
8 Being harsh about cash advance for show (9)
13 Derides reforms when asked (7)
15 Person answering a note with a point to consider (9)
16 Helping a French article make good sense (9)
18 Possibly left with sale brochures (8)
19 Writing about a motorway contract (7)
21 Bread crock upended as a sort of desk (4-3)
22 Oriental rat causing much damage (7)
24 Man reading Arnold novel (6)

NOTES

ACROSS

1 Were these boroughs found in a row in Hyde Park? (6)

5 The low fellow turns his back and there's nothing to it (6)

10 Bad — though Cockney protests otherwise! (7)

11 What a woman butcher might change herself into? (7)

12 Nothing to do with poetry and very distasteful (6)

15 Fake steamer? (6)

16 This landing may result in your getting battered (7)

17 Curling marks letters (4)

18 Something a Canon has that a Dean has not (4)

19 At least one fellow is present in these school premises (7)

20 A super form of shop (4)

22 More than Gog and less than Magog (4)

25 The head's career, perhaps? (7)

27 You can put a great deal of faith into this document (6)

28 Many sailors suffer in this way (6)

31 Any number you like here (7)

32 Tidelet allowed in head (7)

33 Novel hat? (6)

34 Its rights is a heraldic term (6)

DOWN

2 Here it's right for a driver (7)

3 Leaves often swirl in it (6)

4 Saucy young bloods (4)

5 It's clever to rob a Dutch town of its heart (4)

6 Where those in charge have many worries, but all little ones (6)

7 Burial in Nahum's ruin (7)

8 Skilful French direction (6)

9 An artist finds it useful (6)

13 A dangerous place in war-time for a silly fellow to put his top (3-4)

14 A ship in a storm would be flooded without it and its fellows (7)

15 Should a person with a sound head be one to hang about? (7)

20 He's affected to be so pure (6)

21 A fiddler may scarper (7)

23 To execute Spanish fashion (7)

24 At harvest time get the rag out (6)

25 This food should wax well from the start (6)

26 About electric wire now such action is quite automatic (6)

29 Merely (4)

30 Past speed (4)

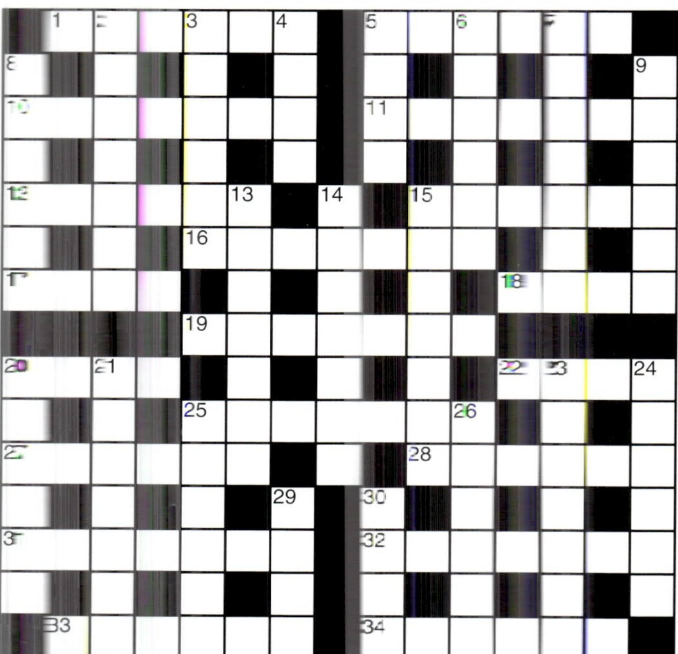

NOTES

SEPTEMBER

MONDAY **17**

TUESDAY **18**

WEDNESDAY **19**

First Quarter

THURSDAY **20**

FRIDAY **21**

SATURDAY **22**

Jewish Day of Atonement (Yom Kippur)

SUNDAY **23**

Autumnal Equinox

Daily Telegraph crossword published in 1952.

WEEK 39 **2007**

SEPTEMBER

24 MONDAY

25 TUESDAY

26 WEDNESDAY

Full Moon

27 THURSDAY

Jewish Festival of Tabernacles (Succoth): First Day

28 FRIDAY

29 SATURDAY

Michaelmas Day

30 SUNDAY

ACROSS

1 Conclusive statement by the ultimate authority (3,4,4)
9 Go too far in trying to correct cameo, so prevent reconstruction (14)
11 Stolen goods left also to be returned (4)
12 Goose that's wild in London (5)
13 Extreme keenness? (4)
16 A way of making Bill work in the house? (8)
17 If it's free, one can say what one likes (6)
19 Eventually observing correct rhythm (2,4)
20 Sidney turns to marriage after separation (8)
22 Donate under pressure (4)
23 Throw into darkness? (5)
24 The one over here belongs to him after end of August (4)
27 Worker, a churchman with reflex action, smashes canoe on the water (9,5)
28 Not much of a surprise from an infant prodigy (5,6)

DOWN

2 Place that's abuzz with signs of great industry? (4,2,8)
3 Fairly recently discovered musical instrument (4)
4 Indicate the space where goods are displayed (8)
5 Penny and I in part of building doing some cleaning (6)
6 Man or lady I left (4)
7 Treat gently when said composer has custody (6,4,4)
8 Operator — but not one working in the theatre (11)
10 Carriage for tired travellers (8-3)
14 Pound for postage (5)
15 Speak gushingly? (5)
18 A ready source of money on the farm? (5-3)
21 I spilt contents on part of the flower (6)
25 Prudish priest on edge (4)
26 Old Bob is able to have a quick look (4)

NOTES

ACROSS

1 Be right, and left as well (7)
5 Boat with less weight (7)
9 After the manner of graduates in a state (7)
10 Means of communication between England and France (7)
11 Not straight and with future too unsettled (3,2,4)
12 Energy needed for a sales campaign (5)
13 Painful reminder of passion when taken to heart (5)
15 In which somebody is travelling flat out? (9)
17 Wonders when the phone is out of order and name has changed (9)
19 Bad organisation (5)
22 Tested when brought before the judge (5)
23 Cold man lacking guile (9)
25 Unsteady dog (7)
26 Mount organist? (7)
27 It measures the strength of the current (7)
28 A number possibly ignore a form of restraint (3,4)

DOWN

1 Confirm a wild animal has escaped (4,3)
2 He begins a race but doesn't finish it (7)
3 Not a big friend of Snow White (5)
4 Domestic fight (9)
5 Cruel way to make a sordid gain (5)
6 Achievement of one who doesn't miss a trick (5,4)
7 Ten shillings to one on "Strain" (7)
8 Release lever, perhaps, that is put in (7)
14 Dashing young men, ardent and inflamed (9)
16 Plea for one to be agreeable and provide financial backing (2,2,5)
17 A girl after a bit of butter for her kneecap (7)
18 Witty saying has some point with animals (7)
20 Possibly slip up providing Spanish and German articles (7)
21 Set off but got no place (4,3)
23 One who rents part of a Yorkshire residence (5)
24 Object to night-work (5)

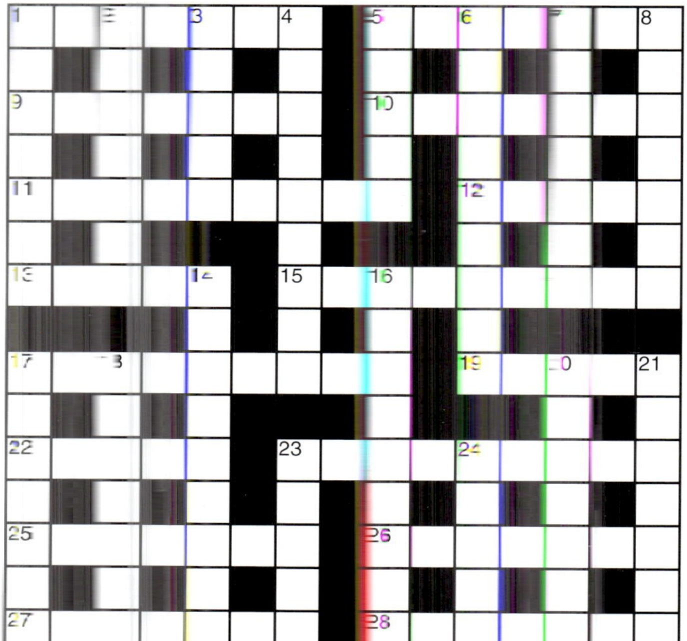

NOTES

OCTOBER

MONDAY **1**

TUESDAY **2**

WEDNESDAY **3**

Last Quarter

THURSDAY **4**

Jewish Festival of Tabernacles (Succoth), Eighth Day

FRIDAY **5**

SATURDAY **6**

SUNDAY **7**

WEEK 41 **2007**

OCTOBER

8 MONDAY

Holiday Canada (Thanksgiving Day)
Holiday USA (Columbus Day)

9 TUESDAY

10 WEDNESDAY

11 THURSDAY

New Moon

12 FRIDAY

13 SATURDAY

14 SUNDAY

ACROSS

1 Apparently pour coffee into hat (2,3,4,2,2)
10 Almost get on board before travel ban (7)
11 Very powerful men I needed after business failure (7)
12 Cost of ring (4)
13 Butter in a can? (5)
14 Bunkumfrom British, hard on the French (4)
17 Sailor lad, lost at sea (3,4)
18 One of "The Mikado"'s fiercest supporters? (7)
19 Reject is unpopular with actors (7)
22 Happy to be not so much in bed (7)
24 Uncomfortable sort of shirt, but it covers one, naturally (4)
25 Reason we hear you entered legal action (5)
26 Girl finds noosed rope a bit short (4)
29 Figure mule ran off (7)
30 For fried dish, better recipe included (7)
31 Urge to go to films, using publicity material (5,8)

DOWN

2 Chewed pen leaked fluid (7)
3 Rent raised, it's said (4)
4 Flag seller? (7)
5 Bird's loud sounds of laughter? (7)
6 Protective clothes one may paint in (4)
7 With narrow horizons — all sea? (7)
8 Close to love? The tiniest bit (4,2,7)
9 Manufacturing sector producing lamps? (5,8)
15 Flat prohibition on a learner (5)
16 Prepare to stop seeing this girl (5)
20 Clipper should be more neat (7)
21 Advertisement for two-wheeler (7)
22 Shy graduate will flush when upset (7)
23 Let's eat out in US city (7)
27 Flower mainly coming from Eire (4)
28 A mountain of a soprano role (4)

NOTES

ACROSS

7 Some, some, some, some golfers may be (9)
8 He, having everything, had virtue — nothing (5)
10 The inclination when a monetary allowance is about to expire (8)
11 Due to a girl being retiring, her social duties may be limited (6)
12 Cow-shed made by engineers (4)
13 Part supplied by a priest taking legal proceedings (8)
16 Secure an item of office furniture (4)
18 He should be able to identify any salt compound (7)
20 Like a horse ready to carry a theologian in an arctic vehicle (7)
22 Appeal to old army girls for marriage basis (4)
24 A leading light in dark proceedings (8)
26 Less pieces of advice (4)
29 In which a groom may find employment is steady (6)
30 Fat once with pig in its own fat (8)
31 Womanly habit of king in burlesque (5)
32 Fiend distributing soup-token (9)

DOWN

1 Sight-seeing expeditions may include it in France (5)
2 I'd go into battle towards the end of the week (6)
3 Desperate advice to the young lover (4)
4 Successfully resist as snobbish suggestion (4,3)
5 A courageous achievement in action but unsuccessful (8)
6 Clear — indication of a lenient magistrate? (5,3)
9 Theory, an aide contrived (4)
14 Network remains (4)
15 Dig deeper for the grave (9)
17 Half the alphabet contains 27 (4)
19 Item in the diet of the insectivorous hen? (8)
21 Size of a type which attracts the reader's attention (8)
23 A very soft way to praise? Hardly (7)
25 To ten supporting a primate (4)
27 Professional weight that's the nub of the matter (6)
28 Colour for putting on (5)

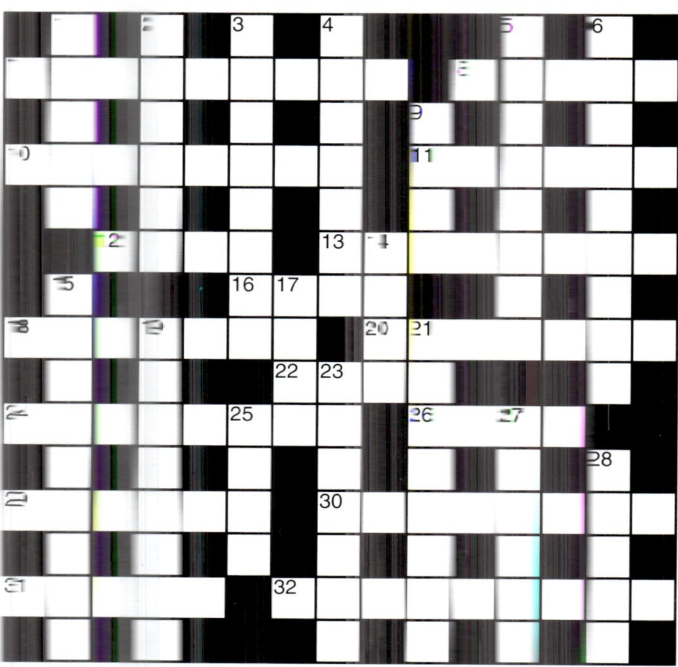

NOTES

OCTOBER

MONDAY **15**

TUESDAY **16**

WEDNESDAY **17**

THURSDAY **18**

FRIDAY **19**

First Quarter

SATURDAY **20**

SUNDAY **21**

Daily Telegraph crossword published in 1973.

WEEK 43

2007

OCTOBER

22 MONDAY

Holiday, New Zealand (Labour Day)

23 TUESDAY

24 WEDNESDAY

United Nations Day

25 THURSDAY

26 FRIDAY

Full Moon

27 SATURDAY

28 SUNDAY

British Summertime ends

ACROSS

1 Trouble on the home front — cleaning woman is repeatedly credited for it (8,6)
9 Takes him a long time, but he finally succeeds (7)
10 Believe he may have done it (7)
11 Object but own it's a mistake (4)
12 It's clear to see, quarrels like this are responsible for lawsuits (10)
14 Eastern ruler left us out to get sunburn (6)
15 Such a curious sheen can heighten the effect and raises the value (8)
17 A topic of conversation with kings, according to Carroll (8)
18 There's hesitation, after all I arranged, to build plant (6)
21 It's dreadfully chilly — rush out rudely in consequence (10)
22 A natural inclination to bias (4)
24 Seems endless, since Ray was taken away outside (7)
25 French painter gets stuck initially, then finds a way in (7)
26 In my view, it's limited (2,3,2,1,3,3)

DOWN

1 Losses may be gains for 12 (7)
2 Workers who go by the book (6,9)
3 The wise man takes his time on a Sunday (4)
4 Offensive remark may be made in lust (6)
5 Provides padding for nothing, copper's shin is broken (8)
6 Basil ate in, by arrangement, but is never satisfied (10)
7 Really, I've reached the point where I can see the uselessness of it all (15)
8 It's a vessel, returned to a state of equilibrium (6)
13 The White House makes an exotic location for Bogart movie (10)
16 Hardy heroine finds the Spanish and French need a small tile for mosaic (8)
17 The seal of distinction (6)
19 It is found, en masse, in the output of this painter (7)
20 Italian mountain troops pin Moslem down (6)
23 Find a grand tomb in an Indian city, and vice versa (4)

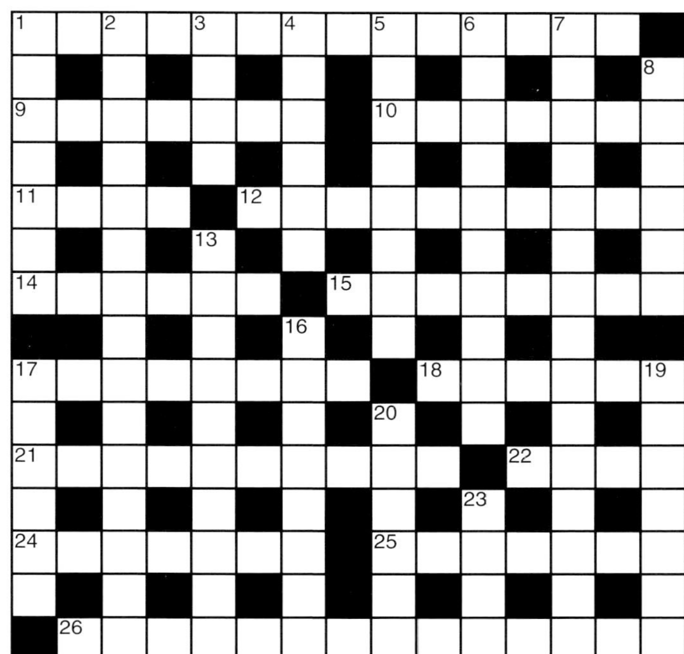

NOTES

ACROSS

1 Fries and reads quickly through the list (4,4)

5 Years when one sees the first bit of rain is coming through (6)

9 Slip back to case the flat involved, but there are dangers (8)

10 Play Nick, the doctor, in it (6)

12 Beats time, which is funny (9)

13 Wins the game against the officers (5)

14 Shoot and get me (4)

16 Working to make the earth better to grow up in (7)

19 Said the right to enter had been established (7)

21 Don't go without a pen (4)

24 Played one's part on account of Ted (5)

25 With a nod, I wave the girl through the entrance (9)

27 "Alight," the author starts, "from a horse-drawn vehicle" (6)

28 Sick, having caught fifty fish (8)

29 Loving and tender, follow round (6)

30 Owing to there being a terrible din outside (3,3,3)

DOWN

1 Somehow spare the time to have something to eat (6)

2 Still fresh, all right (3,3)

3 Pulls the glass up (5)

4 Prepared to fly the sick in (7)

6 Announcing to a meal — or it could be a preamble (4,5)

7 A sincere attack in the counter-argument (8)

8 With a bunch of pals, she had been playing in the water (8)

11 *Second Gear* is a parody (4)

15 The epithet "distant" is taken back (5)

17 Attached because the deal is crooked (8)

18 A hard taskmaster can, in a term, transform (8)

20 Beat! That's thanks to the road being up! (4)

21 Pass a child with a bad limp coming in (7)

22 Further back, get in the way (6)

23 Given to one undercooked, but one's used to that (6)

26 Point out in the silence (5)

NOTES

OCTOBER & NOVEMBER

MONDAY **29**

Holiday, Republic of Ireland

TUESDAY **30**

WEDNESDAY **31**

Hallowe'en

THURSDAY **1**

All Saints' Day
Last Quarter

FRIDAY **2**

SATURDAY **3**

SUNDAY **4**

NOVEMBER

5 MONDAY

Guy Fawkes' Day

6 TUESDAY

7 WEDNESDAY

8 THURSDAY

9 FRIDAY

New Moon

10 SATURDAY

11 SUNDAY

Remembrance Sunday, UK
Holiday, Canada (Remembrance Day) and USA (Veterans' Day)

ACROSS

1 Computer output difficult to follow? (4,4)
5 Foreign side defeated by English slow bowler (6)
9 Watch cricket side in enforced second innings (6-2)
10 Symbol of group or ensemble, mainly inside (6)
11 Show passion for Sue, then, in variety (7)
12 Sort of talk when one's really cold (7)
13 Alternative arrangement in break for refreshments (3,8)
16 In it, one is bound to be in childbed (11)
21 Dead flowers seen on golf courses (7)
22 Acrobat often on bars (7)
23 Syrupy medicine helping to make Felix irritable (6)
24 It is, presumably, only the female that barks (8)
25 Wakes drunkenly after time with sudden, sharp twists (6)
26 American flower for Della to sport we hear (8)

DOWN

1 Blustered and removed man from board (6)
2 Describe the Spanish in charge (6)
3 Came from Pall Mall, we heard (7)
4 Armed person wandering towards concert-goers (11)
6 Rush about wildy and stike servant boy (7)
7 In this case, sailor departed about four (8)
8 Fleet butterflies? (8)
12 Focus attention on dense solution (11)
14 A police investigation leading to conclusive trial (4,4)
15 Is in vice, perhaps, for cutting (8)
17 People need good figures to compete here (3,4)
18 Attitude over a kind of emulsion paint (7)
19 Rugby back in request for something that lines a chest (6)
20 The fat, would you say, of the land? (6)

NOTES

ACROSS

8 The ship's officer who makes the final check? (4)

9 Ben in a hurry! (3)

10 The date no doubt celebrated in the American quarter (6)

11 Stress the breed (6)

12 One might pocket it, especially if demerited! (8)

13 The engineers holding a gift ceremony make petitions (15)

15 Goods vehicles broken by a backward lad, who is one of these? (7)

17 A gee-gee's cry become lean and skinny (7)

20 Fox-chasing university fellows pay for the use of a whole county (15)

23 Listen to repeated expression of approval (4,4)

25 The ragged one who ran around? It's hard to say (6)

26 Chief act before the realm (6)

27 Urgent message that if the ship is lost nothing will be left? (3)

28 The form of vote not unknown in USC! (4)

DOWN

1 The big fight in Sussex (6)

2 Fixed up with a new partner it would seem (8)

3 Colourful decorations that might throw light on some junk! (7,8)

4 Give now! (7)

5 "Confers as caring" (anag.) (in a troubled land) (7,8)

6 Atomic centres (6)

7 Point not raised, though it is of educational value (4)

14 Beer that if followed by gin would be about a quarter-pint (3)

16 Non-consonant trade union, initially speaking (3)

18 Save hide somehow, but only to get the stick! (8)

19 Where one resides so to speak (7)

21 Two sailors joined a terrible fellow (6)

22 Property, two-thirds of which is genuine (6)

24 Neros beheaded for the crowds to see in a famous circus (4)

NOTES

NOVEMBER

MONDAY **12**

TUESDAY **13**

WEDNESDAY **14**

THURSDAY **15**

FRIDAY **16**

SATURDAY **17**

First Quarter

SUNDAY **18**

Daily Telegraph crossword published in 1960.

WEEK 47 2007

NOVEMBER

19 MONDAY

20 TUESDAY

21 WEDNESDAY

22 THURSDAY

Holiday, USA (Thanksgiving Day)

23 FRIDAY

24 SATURDAY

Full Moon

25 SUNDAY

ACROSS

1 Foot's traditional story (6)
4 Silver rig-out on girl in distress (8)
9 Rat swallows a river insect (6)
10 The nearest one can get to a fight (8)
12 The shark needs to exercise (4)
13 Quiet game (5)
14 Depart hurriedly when cast out (4)
17 The Chairman of the Directors could be in deep water (3,9)
20 From pathology Ron turns to the study of man (12)
23 Means of propulsion found on a Roman ship originally (4)
24 Beg for keys (5)
25 Architect helped to make Brighton a showpiece (4)
28 Gloomy start to the music (8)
29 Light breeze round the West (6)
30 Substitutes mine safety officials (8)
31 Violent tale about origin of murder (6)

DOWN

1 Mislaid one's watch and was held up? (4,4)
2 Holding an avaricious attitude (8)
3 Well-dressed beef (4)
5 Painter wins town in local elections (12)
6 Pet that's all the fashion (4)
7 Show how Venice has developed (6)
8 They happen to find an opening in two quarters (6)
11 When fighting men go into the services (6,6)
15 An offer of equality in race matters? (5)
16 Clean servant (5)
18 Kitchen-workers strain to make use of it (8)
19 How to get there, incidentally (2,3,3)
21 Rich enough to have the power to fire (6)
22 Stop and prepare a plan (4,2)
26 Meet in a bar (4)
27 Carefully analyse Kipling's work, in a way (4)

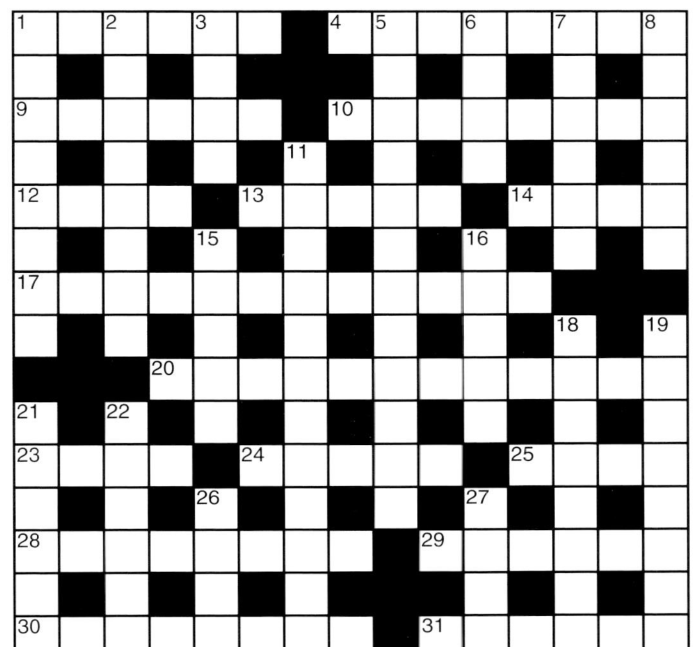

NOTES

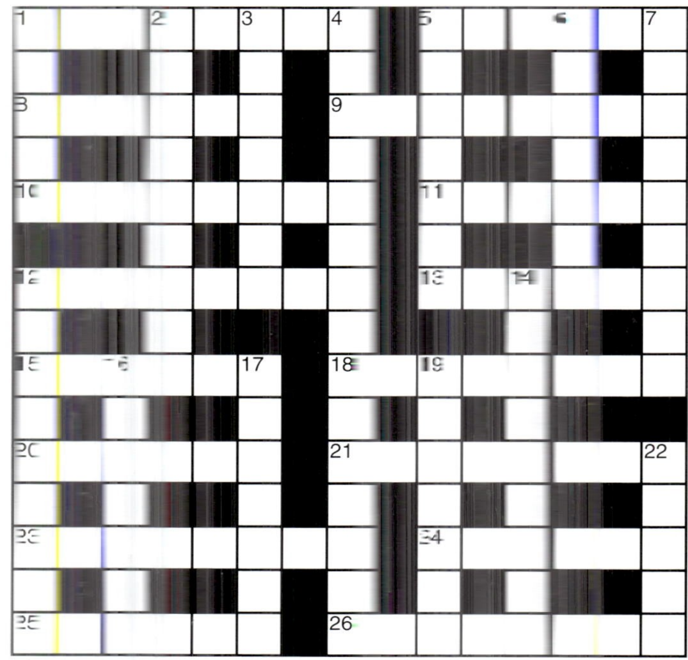

ACROSS

1 Diagram showing pub-crawl route (3-5)
5 Support for new dog (4,2)
8 An office in Paris (6)
9 Happening to fish late in the day (8)
10 Use train (8)
11 Fix aid for driver, a comfortable seat (6)
12 Pointed weapon from mercenary (5,3)
13 Cedars, rotten but not to be touched (6)
15 One hurrying, we hear, to the country (6)
18 Locate record on top (8)
20 To sleep, family provide some linen (6)
21 Deliveries stolen? That's gone too far! (3)
23 Seating erected, but doesn't sit (6,2)
24 Kiss to be among the avengers (6)
25 Nodding, use lousy rhyme (6)
26 Generous gift, note, to the state (8)

DOWN

1 Fur protective cover on the French book (5)
2 Without delight, reel moves off during board game (9)
3 Something wicked in a cup is enjoyable (7)
4 Finally understood small change had to be abandoned (3,5,7)
5 Peace gives solace and delights (7)
6 Indication playwright is open to love (7)
7 One claiming to be peer — trend is worrying (9)
12 Some led strong at first? Tough (4-5)
14 Mashed acorns — it's a French breakfast (9)
16 Singer who can be heard above the rest (7)
17 Prisoners free time? (7)
19 King raised pets and a bird (7)
22 Saw a number working (5)

NOTES

NOVEMBER & DECEMBER

MONDAY **26**

TUESDAY **27**

WEDNESDAY **28**

THURSDAY **29**

FRIDAY **30**

St Andrew's Day

SATURDAY **1**

Last Quarter

SUNDAY **2**

Advent Sunday

WEEK 49 2007

DECEMBER

3 MONDAY

4 TUESDAY

5 WEDNESDAY

Jewish Festival of Chanukah, First Day

6 THURSDAY

7 FRIDAY

8 SATURDAY

9 SUNDAY

New Moon

ACROSS

1 Without resource or expedient — or a smock (9)
8 Out-of-the-way course taken to avoid an engagement (7,6)
11 Water a bunch of flowers (5)
12 Assume as true that I have a job outside (5)
13 Eccentric starting-handle (5)
16 Has her concoction to use again (6)
17 Ancient Scandinavian fellow (6)
18 Initially elected one lady or another (5)
19 She makes her first appearance with no end of danger from rubbish (6)
20 caretaker right on the brink (6)
21 Twenty aggrieved about hundred (5)
24 Word from a song from Cyril (5)
26 Shaver from Alcatraz originally (5)
27 Exercises for divers? (4,9)
28 Suggest remedy for devastated rep with old writer (9)

DOWN

2 Pudding for fast days? (5)
3 Friendly help for a few in the quartet! (6)
4 Burdensome field study (6)
5 Establish a good start on court (3,2)
6 Where bedding plants might spread to another country (4,3,6)
7 Is this business publication for family reading? (5,8)
9 A non-committal position on a horse perhaps (9)
10 Terry, Ian and I deviated from detailed route (9)
13 Musical game (5)
14 Spanish friend in the past went round Michigan (5)
15 Deceitful fellow can be found in church, it is reported (5)
22 But one should not refrain from singing it (6)
23 Mend material on display (6)
25 Change pace and run in an escapade (5)
26 Some are more habitually found in this centre shortly (5)

NOTES

ACROSS

1 Make the unknown known to us (9)
9 Undertaking to eschew flight, or to come back within bounds (6)
10 The stage for some, of course, but this for the rest of the cast (5,4)
11 Seem to have a fruity ending (6)
12 Just a mere necessity for boats like Bluebird making record runs (4,5)
13 Saint competent and firm (6)
17 Fan of a summer afternoon (3)
19 One of the green-eyed familiar to the north of Katmandu (6,6,3)
20 Land this is only a short distance from it (3)
21 The wig needs a fastener in it and attention from a cloth (6)
25 Talk about legal payment: this is a stick-up! (5,4)
26 How the appeal to make a stand was delivered? (6)
27 The CC looking like thunder and getting red in the face, maybe? (9)
28 An adopted offspring of adopted parents (6)
29 There can be no praise for such calumny (9)

DOWN

2 The regular form of Brando's other name (6)
3 He is within the borders as commonly spelt in France (6)
4 She is famous for her good works (5)
5 Can living with in-laws lead to such better understanding? (6,9)
6 One of those small country seats with no backing (4,5)
7 What posh bandits are usually after could be man's bogey (5,4)
8 Helpful with advice to the estranged (9)
14 The trained runners... (9)
15 ...there would be no record time on this (4-5)
16 Vacant air possibly indicating a cerebral vacuum (5,4)
17 A great looking place in Suffolk (3)
18 The voice is part of Cornwall (3)
22 To exert influence I am perhaps to sit (6)
23 Soft drink turns up around the Fleet decks (6)
24 Strong drink is nothing more than a cause of pain (6)

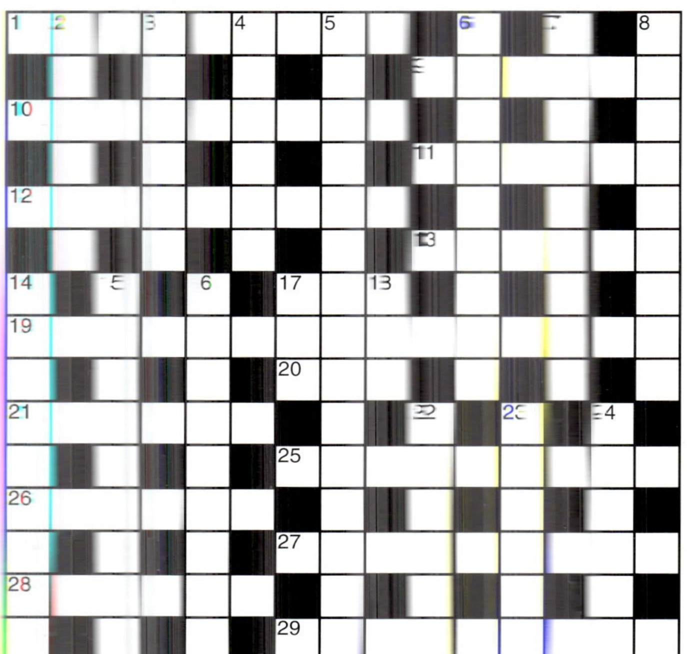

NOTES

DECEMBER

MONDAY **10**

TUESDAY **11**

WEDNESDAY **12**

THURSDAY **13**

FRIDAY **14**

SATURDAY **15**

SUNDAY **16**

Daily Telegraph crossword published in 1957.

WEEK 51 2007

DECEMBER

17 MONDAY

First Quarter

18 TUESDAY

19 WEDNESDAY

20 THURSDAY

21 FRIDAY

22 SATURDAY

Winter Solstice

23 SUNDAY

ACROSS

8, 9 & 10 PE aids lung expansion, so don't hesitate, get into it! (4,3,6)
11 Batman gets the bird (6)
12 Supports FA, since new reshuffle (8)
13 Open display of emotion — many are moved by it (6,9)
15 This chick is, like, yesterday's news (1,3,3)
17 African tribe is first-class — won't be caught in the middle (7)
20 Conclude meetings, which may be of a tertiary nature (5,10)
23 While he's not at the meeting, he's in on it (8)
25 Fifty dance wildly, causing wicked inflammation (6)
26 Prohibition imposed on north-eastern region of Italy (6)
27 Back-chat at the heart of the aga-saga? (3)
28 Arnold Bennett's heroine coined it in India (4)

DOWN

1 Rated X, an adult movie includes scene of Kublai Khan's pleasure dome (6)
2 Intellectually an ally for me, not excluding love in the heart (8)
3 Composure shown by a philatelist is bound to impress (5,10)
4 We left the Far East to find prosperity (7)
5 Easily accessible baggage makes police investigation a doddle (4,3,4,4)
6 That's a novel finish for a trouser-leg! (4-2)
7 Leo's inclined to leer at girls when he's out with the German (4)
14 It can get boring, stuck here in the mating season (3)
16 The pulse of India (3)
18 Put feelers out to Anne about ten-acre plot (8)
19 Square and rugged, but skinny (7)
21 Chap takes an age to reach Hertfordshire town (6)
22 Become less severe about the religious festival (6)
24 Root cause of sugar industry going under (4)

1	2	3	4	5	6	7

NOTES

ACROSS

6 New air hostess turned out to give quality in the main (13)
8 Fan from Tasmania cheering (6)
9 Rainy condition on ring-road is common (8)
10 Sharp rebuke is standard comeback (3)
11 Rub skin off pickle (6)
12 Neat drivers? (8)
14 Footballer busy on crossing (7)
16 Loving call after a party (7)
20 Facade beginning to take a long time (8)
23 Continental woman writes a note about Adam (6)
24 Garland sported by Leicestershire openers? (3)
25 A source in the French game (8)
26 Native American on Java surprisingly (6)
27 Believed university lecture to be a telepathist (7-6)

DOWN

1 Chaff harmful in later years (8)
2 Does one have hard lines writing such poetry? (8)
3 Wasting a prize (7)
4 More cordial for foreign kids? (6)
5 People in wild binges (6)
6 Bobby's hunting-licence? (6,7)
7 Margaret Jones is falling for a soldier (6-5)
13 Couple almost ready to acquire ring? (3)
15 Large sum of money for tea? (3)
17 Top-of-the-table game of matching halves (8)
18 Verdi composition I would note and share again (8)
19 Percussion instrument least used at church (7)
21 Quarrel after midday is limited (6)
22 Grant for delegate (6)

NOTES

DECEMBER

MONDAY **24**

Christmas Eve
Full Moon

TUESDAY **25**

Christmas Day
Holiday, UK, Republic of Ireland,
Canada, USA, Australia and New Zealand

WEDNESDAY **26**

Boxing Day (St Stephen's Day)
Holiday, UK, Republic of Ireland, Canada, Australia and New Zealand

THURSDAY **27**

FRIDAY **28**

SATURDAY **29**

SUNDAY **30**

WEEK 1 2008

DECEMBER & JANUARY

31 MONDAY

New Year's Eve
Last Quarter

1 TUESDAY

New Year's Day
Holiday UK, Republic of Ireland,
Canada, USA, Australia and New Zealand

2 WEDNESDAY

Holiday Scotland and New Zealand

3 THURSDAY

4 FRIDAY

5 SATURDAY

6 SUNDAY

Epiphany

ACROSS

1 Concerned with the landlord being anti-monarchist (10)
6 Beginning well, a member will be genial (4)
10 A strange ring given at farewell in Hawaii (5)
11 Declaration of country people having time (9)
12 Prospect for gold in Central America (8)
13 After a little doggy pal — a terrier maybe (5)
15 A child of three (7)
17 Gets tea out. That could be a bloomer (7)
19 Well-satisfied constituent (7)
21 Show a scholar money — a couple of notes (7)
22 Gain an impression of sound reasoning (5)
24 To create a stir, try imaginative workmanship (8)
27 Expands popular lines (9)
28 Deep depression caused by drain trouble (5)
29 Register British currency first (4)
30 Difficulty made single male shut up about foreign cash (10)

DOWN

1 Stray animal with nothing inside it (4)
2 Trial period for a cricketer no-one backed (9)
3 Do vote with the opposition! (5)
4 Isn't worried over a worker for the moment (7)
5 A hold-up a conservationist body finds hard (7)
7 A man who is representative (5)
8 Beds for fellows wanting hair stuffing (10)
9 Warning the girl in question to carry a key (3,5)
14 Keeps old husband totally idle (5-5)
16 Belgian subjects? (5,3)
18 Weight accorded to a crossing-place in town (9)
20 Beam, having dashed in most elevated (7)
21 He painted lovely pictures of sea-mist, all obscure (7)
23 Steals — prison's indicated! (5)
25 Go astray going over good part of the Middle East (5)
26 Fortitude is called for on icy roads (4)

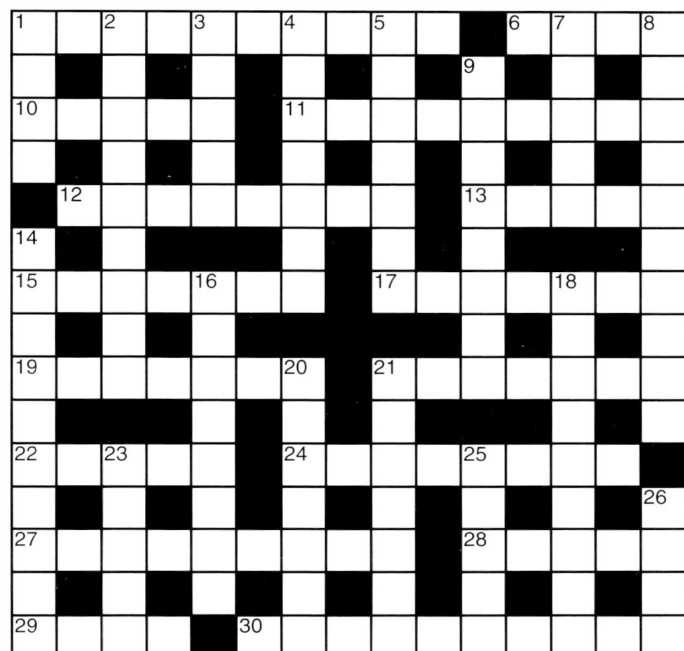

NOTES

EUROPEAN NATIONAL HOLIDAYS 2007

AUSTRIA	Jan. 1, 6; April 8, 9; May 1, 17, 28; June 7; Aug. 15; Oct. 26; Nov. 1; Dec. 8, 25, 26
BELGIUM	Jan. 1; April 8, 9; May 1, 17, 27, 28; July 21; Aug. 15; Nov. 1, 11, 15; Dec. 25, 26
BULGARIA	Jan. 1; March 3; April 9, 21, 28, 31; May 1, 6, 24; Sept. 6, 22; Nov. 1; Dec. 24, 25, 26, 31
CYPRUS	Jan. 1, 6; Feb. 19; March 25; April 1, 6, 8, 9; May 1, 27, 28; Aug. 15; Oct. 1, 28; Dec. 25, 26
CZECH REPUBLIC	Jan. 1; April 8, 9; May 1, 8; July 5, 6; Sept. 28; Oct. 28; Nov. 17; Dec. 24, 25, 26
DENMARK	Jan. 1; April 5, 6, 8, 9; May 4, 17, 27, 28; June 5; Dec. 25, 26
ESTONIA	Jan. 1; Feb. 24; April 6, 8; May 1, 27; June 23, 24; Aug. 20; Dec. 24, 25, 26
FINLAND	Jan. 1, 6; April 6, 8, 9; May 1, 17, 27; June 23; Nov. 3; Dec. 6, 25, 26
FRANCE	Jan. 1; April 8, 9; May 1, 8, 17, 27, 28; July 14; Aug. 15; Nov. 1, 11; Dec. 25
GERMANY	Jan. 1; April 6, 8, 9; May 1, 17, 27, 28; Oct. 3; Dec. 25, 26
GREECE	Jan. 1, 6; Feb. 19; March 25; April 6, 8, 9; May 1, 27, 28; Aug. 15; Oct. 28; Dec. 25, 26
HUNGARY	Jan. 1; March 15; April 8, 9; May 1, 27, 28; Aug. 20; Oct. 23; Nov. 1; Dec. 25, 26
ITALY	Jan. 1, 6; April 8, 9, 25; May 1; June 2; Aug. 15; Nov. 1; Dec. 8, 25, 26
LATVIA	Jan. 1; April 6, 8, 9; May 1, 4; June 23, 24; Nov. 18; Dec. 25, 26, 31
LITHUANIA	Jan. 1; Feb. 16; March 11; April 8, 9; May 1; June 24; July 6; Aug. 15; Nov. 1; Dec. 25, 26
LUXEMBOURG	Jan. 1; Feb. 19; April 8, 9; May 1, 17, 27, 28; June 23; Aug. 15; Nov. 1; Dec. 25, 26
MALTA	Jan. 1; Feb. 10; March 19, 31; April 6, 8; May 1; June 7, 29; Aug. 15; Sept. 8, 21; Dec. 8, 13, 25
NETHERLANDS	Jan. 1; April 6, 8, 9, 30; May 5, 17, 27, 28; Dec. 25, 26
NORWAY	Jan. 1; April 5, 6, 8, 9; May 1, 17, 27, 28; Dec. 25, 26
POLAND	Jan. 1; April 8, 9; May 1, 3; June 7; Aug. 15; Nov. 1, 11; Dec. 25, 26
PORTUGAL	Jan. 1; Feb. 20; April 6, 8, 9, 25; May 1; June 7, 10; Aug. 15; Oct. 5; Nov. 1; Dec. 1, 8, 25
ROMANIA	Jan. 1,2; April 9, 23, 24; May 1; Dec. 1, 25, 26
SLOVAKIA	Jan. 1, 6; April 6, 8, 9; May 1, 8; July 5; Aug. 29; Sept. 1, 15; Nov. 1, 17; Dec. 24, 25, 26
SLOVENIA	Jan. 1, 2; Feb. 8; April 8, 9, 27; May 1, 2, 27; June 27; Aug. 15; Oct. 31; Nov. 1; Dec. 25, 26
SPAIN	Jan. 1, 6; May 19; April 6, 8; May 1, 27; Aug. 15; Oct. 12; Nov. 1; Dec. 6, 8, 25
SWEDEN	Jan. 1, 6; April 6, 8, 9; May 1, 17, 27; June 6, 23; Nov. 3; Dec. 25, 26
SWITZERLAND	Jan. 1; April 6, 8, 9; May 1, 17, 27, 28; Aug. 1; Dec. 25, 26

THE SOLUTIONS

Week 1

ACROSS: 1 Misery, **4** Choppers, **9** Notify, **10** Cucumber, **12** Yank, **13** Ravel, **14** Plan, **17** Obstacle race, **20** Comes in first, **23** Opus, **24** Cruet, **25** Stud, **28** Dragoons, **29** Gaucho, **30** Peerless, **31** Angles. **DOWN: 1** Money-box, **2** Satanism, **3** Raft, **5** House-trained, **6** Paul, **7** Embalm, **8** Spring, **11** Ball-bearings, **15** Baron, **16** Scoff, **18** Protocol, **19** Studious, **21** Hold up, **22** Humane, **26** Goal, **27** Gain.

Week 2

ACROSS: 1 Shipshape, **9** Solace, **10** Enamel, **11** Nail, **12** Resume, **13** Autocracy, **15** Ram, **16** Siesta, **19** Raj, **21** Adelphi, **22** Anguish, **24** Bay, **26** Cavity, **29** Bow, **31** Emotional, **32** Larded, **34** Tuan, **35** Pantry, **36** Noggin, **37** Palestine. **DOWN: 2** Honour, **3** Pompom, **4** Hilary, **5** Panacea, **6** Coleridge, **7** Jaques, **8** Telepathy, **9** Sir, **14** Tare, **17** Barcelona, **18** Apathetic, **19** Rib, **20** Jay, **23** Iron, **25** Ammonia, **27** Virago, **28** Staple, **29** Bonnet, **30** Warren, **33** Dun.

Week 3

ACROSS: 7 Clearance, **8** Count, **10** Danger, **11** Drop-leaf, **12** Listed, **14** Berate, **16** Pass, **17** Brace, **18** Wild, **19** Sparks, **21** Nobody, **24** Equality, **26** Rooted, **27** Given, **28** By No means. **DOWN: 1** Bleak, **2** Bargains, **3** Parrot, **4** Acid, **5** Howler, **6** Infantile, **9** Double, **13** Drain, **15** Damp squib, **17** Buskin, **18** Wide open, **20** Reader, **22** Barrow, **23** Seine, **25** Yo-yo.

Week 4

ACROSS: 1 Cashier, **5** Clothes, **9** Circled, **10** Inferno, **11** Poker-face, **12** Otter, **13** Turns, **15** Pea-souper, **17** Saltpetre, **19** Rebut, **22** Alamo, **23** Mediation, **25** Tuition, **26** Terrace, **27** Engaged, **28** Lenient. **DOWN: 1** Cockpit, **2** Striker, **3** Idler, **4** Red carpet, **5** Chide, **6** Off-colour, **7** Hardtop, **8** Scourer, **14** Supposing, **16** Anecdota, **17** Startle, **18** Leading, **20** Brigade, **21** Tangent, **23** Mined, **24** Apron.

Week 5

ACROSS: 1 Dowel, **4** Pipe dream, **9** Fulsome, **11** Airmail, **12** Rood, **13** Might, **14** Riga, **17** Safety-curtain, **19** Recapitulates, **21** Elms, **22** Flags, **23** Carp, **26** Tsarina, **27** Tuneful, **28** Antipasto, **29** Holst. **DOWN: 1** Deforests, **2** Well-off, **3** Look, **5** Play hard to get, **6** Derv, **7** Elation, **8** Malta, **10** Episcopalians, **15** Stuck, **16** Daily, **18** Test-pilot, **19** Remnant, **20** Tearful, **21** Extra, **24** Limp, **25** Inch.

Week 6

ACROSS: 1 Covert, **4** Amphibia, **9** Malice, **10** Landlord, **12** Tonga, **13** Fishplate, **15** Nor, **16** Swing, **17** All but, **22** Leaden, **24** Doorn, **27** The, **28** Heartache, **31** Right, **32** Specific, **33** Johore, **34** Starfish, **35** Beasts. **DOWN: 1** Comatose, **2** Valencia, **3** Rectangle, **5** Means, **6** Had up, **7** Bhopal, **8** Andrew, **11** Afraid, **14** Hub, **18** Lenten, **19** Underdone, **20** Gorgeous, **21** Knotless, **23** ARA, **25** Thesis, **26** Camera, **29** Thief, **30** Caius.

Week 7

ACROSS: 1 Sea-rover, **5** Lancet, **9** Contends, **10** Recall, **11** Overland, **12** Miller, **14** Renovation, **18** Confidence, **22** Brogue, **23** Reveille, **24** Arenas, **25** Strangle, **26** Dashed, **27** Brunette. **DOWN: 1** Sector, **2** Arnhem, **3** Openly, **4** Endangered, **6** American, **7** Chaplain, **8** Tolerant, **13** Dorchester, **15** Scabbard, **16** Snoopers, **17** Misusage, **19** Remain, **20** Slight, **21** Delete.

Week 8

ACROSS: 1 & 9 As clear as crystal, **10** Quarter, **11** Not true, **12** Pakistani, **14** Acanthus, **15** Backer, **17** Melrose, **20** Priest, **23** Interest, **25** Certified, **26** Anarchy, **27** Pandora, **28** Unhitch, **29** Enchilada. **DOWN: 2 & 15** Snug as a bug in a rug, **3** Lerwick, **4** Aperture, **5** Scenic, **6** Bystander, **7** Starchy, **8** Aldershot, **13** Narrate, **15** See 2, **16** Embrocate, **18** Spot cash, **19** Attache, **21** Infidel, **22** Speared, **24** Scythe.

Week 9

ACROSS: 1 Mobile library, **10** Untried, **11** Pursuit, **12** Slot, **13** Break, **14** Dali, **17** Nosegay, **18** Handbag, **19** Staunch, **22** Tea-leaf, **24** Apex, **25** Manse, **26** Free, **29** Icicles, **30** Ushered, **31** Salvation Army. **DOWN: 2** Options, **3** Ibis, **4** Elderly, **5** Impeach, **6** Rare, **7** Rhubarb, **8** Puts ones oar in, **9** String of beads, **15** Aging, **16** Sneak, **20** America, **21** Headset, **22** Testudo, **23** Ear-drum, **27** Slav, **28** Whoa.

Week 10

ACROSS: 1 Robot, **4** First-hand, **9** Fondles, **11** Panicky, **12** Exit, **13** Tabby, **14** Weed, **17** High-and-mighty, **19** Decontaminate, **21** Base, **22** Solid, **23** Prim, **26** Edified, **27** Martian, **28** High horse, **29** Energy. **DOWN: 1** Refresher, **2** Bunting, **3** Tell, **5** Republicanism, **6** Tank, **7** Archery, **8** Dryad, **10** Standing order, **15** Match, **16** Chain, **18** Even money, **19** Dashing, **20** Airline, **21** Beech, **24** Fish, **25** Free.

Week 11

ACROSS: 1 Hire-purchase, **8** Missile, **9** Charges, **12** Recto, **13** Salve, **14** Cuba, **17** Sweeter, **18** Polish, **19** Nostrum, **22** Pay cash, **24** Eire, **25** Snare, **26** Ammo, **29** Theorem, **31** Overdue, **32** Supermarkets. **DOWN: 1** Possible, **2** Reir, **3** Prelacy, **4** Recover, **5** Head, **6** Eye, **7** Imprisonment, **10** Clues, **11** Sharp shooter, **15** Stare, **16** Player, **20** Serge, **21** Minimum, **22** Parlour, **23** Armecas, **27** Tree, **28** Cede, **30** [illegible]

Week 12

ACROSS: 1 Housemaid's knee, **9** Required, **10** Run-up, **11** Alec, **13** Detestable, **15** Essaying, **16** Seized, **18** Orally, **20** Panorama, **23** Lady chapel, **24** Mall, **25** Corgi, **27** Fresco, **28** Warning signals. **DOWN: 2** Useless, **3** Etui, **4** Agreeing, **5** Dodgem, **6** Karate chop, **7** Ennoble, **8** [illegible], **11** Take pot luck, **14** By-election, **17** Laterness, **19** Andorra, **21** Amanita, **22** Baffin, **25** Ergo.

Week 13

ACROSS: 1 Allowed, **5** Bill, **9** Birds of paradise, **10** Reed, **11** Taste, **12** Seek, **15** Attract, **16** Deadpan, **17** Bracing, **19** Marches, **21** Calf, **22** Block, **23** Agra, **26** Coffee-table book, **27** Spin, **28** Epistle. **DOWN: 1** Alberta, **2** Larger than life, **3** Wash, **4** Defiant, **5** Blasted, **6** Lead, **7** Dervish, **8** Give up the ghost, **13** Fakir, **14** Tarry, **17** Beadle, **18** Gelatin, **19** Macabre, **20** Shackle, **24** Keep, **25** Semi.

Week 14

ACROSS: 1 Sea-green, **5** Across, **9** Adorable, **10** Camera, **12** Carton, **13** Post paid, **15** Respite, **16** Lean, **20** Ears, **21** Monarch, **25** Obtained, **26** Clever, **28** Theory, **29** Fathom, **30** Rasher, **31** Dearness. **DOWN: 1** Search, **2** Aboard, **3** Reasoned, **4** Ella, **6** Chaste, **7** Operates, **8** Scalding, **11** Penny, **14** Opposed, **17** Reporter, **18** Fritter, **19** Sculptor, **22** Pierce, **23** Evince, **24** Primer, **27** Else.

Week 15

ACROSS: 1 Adjudicate, **6** Scab, **9** Forefinger, **10** Aria, **12** Learn a lesson, **15** Craven, **16** Vulcan, **18** Essaying, **19** Verses, **21** Turn a deaf ear, **24** Bump, **25** Empiricism, **26** Erne, **27** Exaggerate. **DOWN: 1** Asia, **2** July, **3** Differential, **4** Canard, **5** Thematic, **7** Christened, **8** Brainstorm, **11** Regenerative, **13** Acceptable, **14** [illegible], **17** Intermix, **20** Offing, **22** Lisa, **23** Smee.

Week 16

ACROSS: 1 End of term, **9** Lupine, **10** Spare ribs, **11** Amber, **12** Transmits, **13** Ashram, **17** Era, **19** Leander, **20** Let down, **21** Ape, **23** Carols, **27** Underline, **28** Ledger, **29** Takes a toss, **30** Scouse, **31** Sets aside. **DOWN: 2** Napery, **3** Damage, **4** Thrums, **5** Ribston, **6** Bulrushes, **7** Liverpool, **8** Pertinent, **14** Blacklist, **15** Sacred cow, **16** Exercise, **17** Era, **18** Ale, **22** Pancake, **24** Recess, **25** Pates, **26** Unused.

Week 17

ACROSS: 1 Drop out, **5** Thrusts, **9** Ailment, **10** Lying-in, **11** Short slip, **12** Shore, **13** Their, **15** Graphology, **17** Halitosis, **19** Erica, **22** Donor, **23** Greatness, **25** Imitate, **26** Garotte, **27** Negated, **28** Release. **DOWN: 1** [illegible], **2** Only one, **3** Over, **4** Total loss, **5** Tulip, **6** [illegible], **7** Signora, **8** Sneeze, **14** Retardant, **16** Passenger, **17** Harrier, **18** Landing, **20** Inertia, **21** Austere, **23** Greed, **24** Tyrol.

Week 18

ACROSS: 1 Estimating, **6** Stem, **9** Honed, **10** Christian, **12** Bite the bullet, **14** Evermore, **15** Trader, **17** Entrap, **19** Eight bucks, **21** Evolutionists, **24** Desperado, **25** Image, **26** Mass, **27** Plate glass. **DOWN: 1** Echo, **2** Tenable, **3** Made to measure, **4** Taciturn, **5** Nurse, **7** Trifled, **8** Monetarism, **11** Square-bashing, **13** Referendum, **16** Signature, **18** Taoists, **20** Cassette, **22** In all, **23** Lens.

Week 19

ACROSS: 1 Cheval glass, **9** Quot, **10** Portmanteau, **11** Iona, **12** Psalm, **15** Shred, **17** Owl, **18** Beam, **19** Hug, **21** Chill, **22** Lemur, **23** Dab, **26** Part, **27** Ass, **28** Phial, **30** Spat, **33** Tithe, **35** Rectangular, **36** Tour, **37** Herring bone. **DOWN: 2** Hoots, **3** Vital, **4** Loam, **5** Leech, **6** Squid, **7** Gendarme, **8** Stock market, **12** Precipitate, **13** Abstraction, **14** Mould, **15** Sly, **16** Emu, **20** Gloss, **24** Ash, **25** Fat, **28** Pert, **29** Aster, **31** Plumb, **32** Learn, **34** [illegible]

Week 20

ACROSS: 1 Habit, **4** Castaway, **10** Tactile, **11** Halogen, **12** Less, **13** Stare, **14** Pass, **17** Experimentally, **19** Sits on the fence, **22 & 23** Andy Pandy, **24** Asia, **27** Piccadilly, **28** Facets, **29** La Société, **30** Tatt. **DOWN: 1** Hobbies, **2** Backs up, **3** Trio, **5** A shot in the dark, **6** Tit, **7** Wagtail, **8** Yankee, **9** Sentimentalist, **15** Trust, **16** Gaffe, **18** Strategy, **20** Induces, **21** Nascent, **22** Appal, **25** Lair, **26** Boat.

Week 21

ACROSS: 1 Cuban, **4** Comedians, **9** Tableau, **11** Updated, **12** Load, **13** Idaho, **14** Isle, **17** Police station, **19** Clarinetists, **21** Cork, **22** Plain, **23** View, **26** Pronoun, **27** Garbage, **28** Amsterdam, **29** Coke. **DOWN: 1** Catalepsy, **2** Bobtail, **3** Noes, **5** Mouth-watering, **6** Dodo, **7** Artisan, **8** Sedge, **10** Undisciplined, **15** Scrap, **16** Wilt, **18** Elsewhere, **19** Gardens, **20** Spinach, **21** Copra, **24** Ooze, **25** Trio.

Week 22

ACROSS: 1 Manicurist, **9** Mead, **10** Terminator, **11** Reveal, **12** Settled, **15** Sea-legs, **16** Donor, **17** Rues, **18** Race, **19** Henna, **21** Toaster, **22** Dissent, **24** Heifer, **27** Ill-feeling, **28** Need, **29** Goods-train. **DOWN: 2** Amen, **3** Inmost, **4** Unnamed, **5** Iota, **6** Terrier, **7** Decelerate, **8** Adolescent, **12** Scratching, **13** The Marines, **14** Dover, **15** Sound, **19** Herring, **20** Airless, **23** Staler, **25** Alto, **26** Anti.

Week 23

ACROSS: 1 Clark Gable, **6** Ibis, **9** Slow-motion, **10** Peel, **13** Red flag, **15** Cartel, **16** Harrow, **17** The tower of Babel, **18** Espial, **20** Ignite, **21** Lovable, **22** Even, **25** Wire-cutter, **26** Soho, **27** Another day. **DOWN: 1** Cast, **2** Atom, **3** Kummel, **4** Act of Parliament, **5** Loofah, **7** Brer Rabbit, **8** Self-willed, **11** Scatheless, **12** Free speech, **13** Removal, **14** Gamboge, **19** Lotion, **20** Illume, **23** Stud, **24** Dray.

Week 24

ACROSS: 1 Foothill, **5** Rhodes, **9** Drainage, **10** Visage, **11** Look out, **12** Buckram, **13** Presentable, **16** Baker's dozen, **21** Reposed, **22** Benefit, **23** Voiced, **24** Doornail, **25** Niggle, **26** Skinhead. **DOWN: 1** Fiddle, **2** Orator, **3** Hencoop, **4** Light-headed, **6** Haircut, **7** Diatribe, **8** Steamier, **12** Breeze-block, **14** Aberavon, **15** Skipping, **17** Russell, **18** Non-iron, **19** Aflame, **20** Stolid.

Week 25

ACROSS: 1 Put a stop to, **9** Scar, **10** Enterprise, **11** Recoup, **12** Winding, **15** Sworn in, **16** Grate, **17** Sets, **18** Taxi, **19** Tempt, **21** Yule-log, **22** Swarthy, **24** Aerial, **27** Bill of fare, **28** Hash, **29** Red herring. **DOWN: 2** Urns, **3** Age-old, **4** Tipping, **5** Pail, **6** Overawe, **7** Accountant, **8** Propensity, **12** Wishy-washy, **13** Nettle rash, **14** Grieg, **15** Stops, **19** Toll-bar, **20** Twosome, **23** Roofer, **25** Clod, **26** Iron.

Week 26

ACROSS: 1 Capering, **9** Obituary, **10** Snap, **11** Exaggeration, **13** Anathema, **15** Dances, **16** Lent, **17** Brest, **18** Ohms, **20** School, **21** Preening, **23** Presbyterian, **26** Oils, **27** Sardines, **28** Trade gap. **DOWN: 2** Announce, **3** Expectations, **4** In case, **5** Gong, **6** Microdot, **7** Taxi, **8** Gymnasts, **12** Ten-pound note, **14** Ate up, **16** Last post, **17** Bullying, **19** Mongolia, **22** Enigma, **24** Eire, **25** Erst.

Week 27

ACROSS: 1 Dicky, **4** Round trip, **8** Ripen, **9** Vehemence, **11** Dirk, **12** Blare, **13** Shod, **16** Ghetto-blaster, **19** Lotus position, **20** Mace, **22** Babel, **23** Peke, **26** Archetype, **27** Tripe, **28** Sheathing, **29** Guest. **DOWN: 1** Daredevil, **2** Copyright, **3** Yank, **4** Revolutionary, **5** Dumb, **6** Ranch, **7** Pseud, **10** Hard-boiled egg, **14** Beast, **15** Cavil, **17** Tangerine, **18** Represent, **20** Means, **21** Cache, **24** Best, **25** Stag.

Week 28

ACROSS: 1 Fiancé, **4** Sculptor, **10** Reinforce, **11** Siren, **12** Chaotic, **13** Terrace, **14** Sheer, **15** Defector, **18** Retailer, **20** Pasta, **23** Neglect, **25** Wastage, **26** Treat, **27** Air pocket, **28** Hedonist, **29** Meanly. **DOWN: 1** Forecast, **2** Agitate, **3** Cafeteria, **5** Chest of drawers, **6** Loser, **7** Tornado, **8** Ranger, **9** Crocodile tears, **16** Copestone, **17** Tapestry, **19** Egghead, **21** Slacken, **22** Snitch, **24** Eaten.

Week 29

ACROSS: 1 Keep out of the way, **9** Intricate, **10** Raise, **11** Hence, **12** Unclothed, **13** Sleighs, **14** Mouser, **16** Cockle, **18** Dentists, **22** Road shows, **23** Eyrie, **24** Obeli, **25** Clarionet, **26** Youth hostellers. **DOWN: 1** Knights, **2** Entente, **3** Oliver Goldsmith, **4** Traducer, **5** Fresco, **6** Harrow on the Hill, **7** Writhes, **8** Yielder, **15** Redstart, **16** Cursory, **17** Chateau, **19** Syringe, **20** Sleuths, **21** Poncho.

Week 30

ACROSS: 1 Split second, **9** Tolerance, **10** Naomi, **11** Amends, **12** Aspersed, **13** Sister, **15** Persuade, **18** Sinister, **19** Wait up, **21** Abrasion, **23** Change, **26** Ideal, **27** Tide-table, **28** Elderliness. **DOWN: 1** Satraps, **2** Lille, **3** Tiredness, **4** Erne, **5** Overseen, **6** Donne, **7** Dwindle, **8** Constant, **14** Sundries, **16** Spaghetti, **17** Revolted, **18** Slaving, **20** Peeress, **22** Solve, **24** Noble, **25** Oder.

Week 31

ACROSS: 1 Pick-up, **4** Scalawag, **10** Nepal, **11** Innkeeper, **12** Frigate, **13** Trodden, **14** Racing calendar, **17** Political party, **21** Arsenic, **23** Insider, **24** About-turn, **25** Wring, **26** Antidote, **27** Oregon. **DOWN: 1** Pinafore, **2** Capriccio, **3** Unlearn, **5** Constellations, **6** Lie down, **7** Wiped, **8** Gerona, **9** Silence in court, **15** Abridging, **16** Hydrogen, **18** Ignited, **19** Postwar, **20** Panama, **22** Sport.

Week 32

ACROSS: 6 Bank overdraft, **8** Rubber, **9** Passport, **10** Ida, **11** Stated, **12** Gangster, **14** Hurdler, **16** Round up, **20** Assembly, **23** Timbre, **24** Per, **25** Literati, **26** Instep, **27** No great shakes. **DOWN: 1** Unabated, **2** Porridge, **3** Seepage, **4** Edison, **5** Campus, **6** Blunt question, **7** Three-quarters, **13** Gnu, **15** Lam, **17** Outright, **18** Namesake, **19** Typists, **21** Energy, **22** Biased.

Week 33

ACROSS: 1 Fingerprints, **8** [illegible]wind, **9** [illegible], **11** [illegible], **12** Shannon, **13** Niger, **14** Ill at ease, **16** Whirligig, **19** Gibes, **21** Thought, **23** Tooting, **24** [illegible], **25** [illegible], **26** [illegible] Place. **DOWN: 1** Failing, **2** Neither, **3** Endearing, **4** Pans, **5** Implant, **6** Titania, **7** Milk and water, **10** Danger signal, **15** Lightship, **17** [illegible], **18** Lugsail, **19** Georgia, **20** Brittle, **22** Titan.

Week 34

ACROSS: 1 Statesman, **9** No more, **10** [illegible], **11** [illegible], **12** Home Guard, **13** [illegible], **17** Lid, **19** The queen of clubs, **20** Gag, **21** Cavell, **25** [illegible], **26** [illegible], **27** [illegible], **28** Lodger, **29** [illegible]. **DOWN: 2** Tripod, **3** [illegible], **4** Sprout, **5** A storm in a teacup, **6** [illegible], **7** Royal blue, **8** Headdress, **14** Stockpile, **15** [illegible], **16** Qualified, **17** Leg, **18** Dog, **22** Motion, **23** [illegible], **24** [illegible].

Week 35

ACROSS: 1 Bats, **3** Cue, **5** Hang-up, **8** [illegible], **9** [illegible], **10** Hell-fire, **11** Switch, **12** Chambers, **13** [illegible], **15** Vernal, **18** Evictors, **20** Locke, **21** In a clear, **23** In charge, **24** If only, **25** Toe-cap, **26** [illegible], **27** [illegible]. **DOWN: 1** Brash, **2** Stableman, **3** Caddice, **4** Express delivery, **5** Headset, **6** Granted, **7** [illegible], **12** [illegible], **14** [illegible], **16** Recycle, **17** [illegible] drop, **19** Iranian, **22** Mayan.

Week 36

ACROSS: 1 Accompany, **8** Custodianship, **11** [illegible], **12** [illegible], **13** Beat, **16** [illegible], **17** Answer, **18** Ravel, **19** Leeway, **20** Lintel, **21** Lusty, **24** [illegible], **26** [illegible], **27** Precious metal, **28** Tradesman. **DOWN: 2** [illegible], **3** Ordeal, **4** Plasma, **5** Nasty, **6** Juvenile court, **7** Nightwatchman, **9** [illegible], **10** Hour-glass, **13** Beryl, **14** Eaves, **15** [illegible], **22** Uphold, **23** Thesis, **25** Pacer, **26** Arena.

Week 37

ACROSS: 1 Proposers, **9** Close-up, **10** [illegible], **11** [illegible], **12** Esplanade, **14** Enquired, **15** [illegible], **17** [illegible], **20** Eerie, **23** Portière, **25** Odd fellow, **26** Nominal, **27** [illegible], **28** Epsilon, **29** Dissipate. **DOWN: 2** [illegible], **3** Farolee, **4** Stagnate, **5** Screen, **6** Concourse, **7** [illegible], **8** [illegible], **13** Desired, **15** Responder, **16** [illegible], **18** Leaflets, **19** Promise, **21** Roll-top, **22** Eroded, **24** [illegible].

Week 38

ACROSS: 1 Rotten, **5** Dacoit, **10** Defiant, **11** Fresher, **12** [illegible], **15** Shammy, **16** Pancake, **17** [illegible], **18** [illegible], **19** Chapels, **20** Pooh, **22** Agog, **25** Caterer, **27** [illegible], **29** Regret, **31** Unseen, **32** Palette, **33** [illegible], **34** [illegible]. **DOWN: 2** Offside, **3** Teacup, **4** Nuts, **5** Deft, **6** Cache, **7** Inhuman, **8** [illegible], **9** Crayon, **13** [illegible], **14** [illegible], **18** Skulker, **20** Poseur, **21** Scraper, **23** Garotte, **24** [illegible], **25** [illegible], **26** Reflex, **29** Only, **30** [illegible].

Week 39

ACROSS: 1 The last word, **9** Overcompensate, **11** Lost, **12** Brent, **13** Edge, **16** [illegible], **17** [illegible], **19** In time, **20** Disunion, **22** Give, **23** Pitch, **24** This, **27** Antarctic Ocean, **28** Smallwonder. **DOWN: 2** Hive of activity, **3** Lyre, **4** Showroom, **5** Wiping, **6** Rene, **7** Handle with care, **8** [illegible], **10** Sleeping-car, **14** [illegible], **15** [illegible], **18** Milch-cow, **21** Petil, **25** Prim, **26** Scan.

Week 40

ACROSS: 1 Besides, **5** Lighter, **9** Alabama, **10** Channel, **11** Out of true, **12** Drive, **13** [illegible], **15** Ambulance, **17** Phenomena, **19** Mafia, **22** Tried, **23** [illegible], **25** [illegible], **26** Grinder, **27** Ammeter, **28** Leg-iron. **DOWN: 1** Bear out, **2** Starter, **3** Dwarf, **4** Staircase, **5** Lucre, **6** [illegible], **7** [illegible], **8** Relieve, **14** [illegible], **16** [illegible], **17** Patella, **18** [illegible], **20** Fielder, **21** [illegible], **23** [illegible], **24** [illegible].

Week 41

ACROSS: 1 On the face of it, **10** [illegible], **11** [illegible], **12** Toll, **13** Bill, **14** Blah, **17** [illegible], **18** Samurai, **19** Outcast, **22** Blessed, **24** Hair, **25** Cause, **26** [illegible], **28** Numeral, **30** [illegible], **31** Press releases. **DOWN: 2** [illegible], **3** Hie, **4** Florist, **5** Cackles, **6** Oils, **7** Insular, **8** [illegible], **9** Light industry, **15** Banal, **16** Amber, **20** [illegible], **21** Trailer, **22** Bashful, **23** Seattle, **27** Iris, **28** Aida.

Week 42

ACROSS: 7 Foursomes, **8** [illegible], **10** Gradient, **11** [illegible], **12** Byre, **13** Fraction, **16** Safe, **18** Analyst, **20** Saddled, **22** Oats, **24** Headlamp, **26** Tips, **29** Stable, **30** [illegible], **31** [illegible], **32** Outspoken. **DOWN: 1** [illegible], **2** Friday, **3** Hopeless, **4** Bear off, **5** Defeated, **6** Bounce over, **9** [illegible], **14** Rest, **15** Undertake, **17** Atom, **19** Ladybird, **21** Asterisk, **23** Applaud, **25** Apex, **27** Proton, **28** Green.

Week 43

ACROSS: 1 Domestic crisis, **9** Manager, **10** [illegible], **11** [illegible], **12** Plaintiffs, **14** Sultan, **15** Eminence, **17** Cabbages, **18** Allium, **21** Churlishly, **22** Bent, **24** Eternal, **25** [illegible], **26** As far as I can see. **DOWN: 1** Damages, **2** Manual labourers, **3** Sage, **4** Insult, **5** Cushions, **6** Insatiable, **7** [illegible] effectiveness, **8** Stasis, **13** Casablanca, **16** [illegible], **17** Cachet, **19** Matisse, **20** Alpini, **23** Agra.

Week 44

ACROSS: 1 Runs down, **5** Sports, **9** Pitfalls, **10** Gambol, **12** Slapstick, **13** Mates, **14** Twig, **16** Tillage, **19** Started, **21** Stay, **24** Acted, **25** Admission, **27** Landau, **28** Flounder, **29** Doting, **30** In the red. **DOWN: 1** Repast, **2** Not bad, **3** Draws, **4** Willing, **6** Pear Melba, **7** Rebuttal, **8** Splashed, **11** Skit, **15** Withdrawn, **17** Assailed **18** Martinet, **20** Drat, **21** Simplon, **22** Hinder, **23** Inured, **26** South.

Week 45

ACROSS: 1 Hard copy, **5** Armada, **9** Follow-on, **10** Emblem, **11** Enthuse, **12** Chatter, **13** Tea interval, **16** Confinement, **21** Drivers, **22** Tumbler, **23** Elixir, **24** Malemute, **25** Tweaks, **26** Delaware. **DOWN: 1** Huffed, **2** Relate, **3** Croquet, **4** Promenaders, **6** Rampage, **7** Ablative, **8** Admirals, **12** Concentrate, **14** Acid test, **15** Incisive **17** Ice rink, **18** Tempera, **19** Pleura, **20** Greece.

Week 46

ACROSS: 8 Mate, **9** Hur, **10** Fourth, **11** Strain, **12** Shilling, **13** Representations, **15** Vandals **17** Scraggy, **20** Huntingdonshire, **23** Hear hear, **25** Rascal, **26** Domain, **27** SOS, **28** Veto. **DOWN: 1** Battle, **2** Repaired, **3** Chinese lanterns, **4** Present, **5** African congress, **6** Nuclei, **7** Eton, **14** Nog, **16** AEU, **18** Adhesive, **19** Address, **21** Tartar, **22** Realty, **24** Eros.

Week 47

ACROSS: 1 Legend, **4** Aggrieve, **9** Scarab, **10** Ringside, **12** Tope, **13** Whist, **14** Scat, **17** Man overboard, **20** Anthropology, **23** Oars, **24** Cadge, **25** Nash, **28** Downbeat, **29** Window, **30** Deputies, **31** Stormy. **DOWN: 1** Lost time, **2** Grasping, **3** Neat, **5** Gainsborough, **6** Rage, **7** Evince, **8** Events, **11** Church parade, **15** Evens, **16** Groom, **18** Colander, **19** By the way, **21** Loaded, **22** Draw up, **26** Abut, **27** Sift.

Week 48

ACROSS: 1 Bar-chart, **5** Prop up, **8** Bureau, **9** Eventide, **10** Exercise, **11** Settee, **12** Hired gun, **13** Sacred, **15** Russia, **18** Discover, **20** Napkin, **21** Overshot, **23** Stands up, **24** Heaven, **25** Drowsy, **26** Donation. **DOWN: 1** Bible, **2** Cheerless, **3** Amusing, **4** The penny dropped, **5** Pleases, **6** Pointer, **7** Pretender, **12** Hard-nosed, **14** Croissant, **16** Soprano, **17** Amnesty, **19** Stephen, **22** Tenon.

Week 49

ACROSS: 1 Shiftless, **8** Evasive action, **11** Spray, **12** Posit, **13** Crank, **16** Rehash, **17** Norman, **18** Eliza, **19** Debris, **20** Verger, **21** Score, **24** Lyric, **26** Razor, **27** Deep breathing, **28** Prescribe. **DOWN: 2** Hasty, **3** Favour, **4** Leaden, **5** Set up, **6** Over the border, **7** House magazine, **9** Astraddle, **10** Itinerary, **13** Chess, **14** Amigo **15** Knave **22** Chorus, **23** Repair, **25** Caper, **26** Rehab.

Week 50

ACROSS: 1 Introduce, **9** Parole, **10** Green room, **11** Appear, **12** Calm water, **13** Stable, **17** Era, **19** Little yellow god, **20** Ell, **21** Wiping, **25** Stamp duty, **26** Orally, **27** Colouring, **28** Cuckoo, **29** Aspersion. **DOWN: 2** Normal, **3** Rheims, **4** Dorcas, **5** Closer relations, **6** Camp stool, **7** Money bags, **8** Befriends, **14** Slowcoach, **15** Stop-watch, **16** Blank look, **17** Eye, **18** All, **22** Impose, **23** Adorns, **24** Stingo.

Week 51

ACROSS: 8, 9 & 10 Take the plunge, **11** Bantam, **12** Finances, **13** Public transport, **15** Aged, old, **17** Ashanti, **20** Close encounters, **23** Absentia, **25** Candle, **26** Veneto, **27** Gas, **28** Anna. **DOWN: 1** Xanadu, **2** Mentally, **3** Stamp collection, **4** Welfare, **5** Open and shut case, **6** Turn-up, **7** Ogle, **14** Rut, **16** Dal, **18** Antennae, **19** Scraggy, **21** Steven, **22** Relent, **24** Beet.

Week 52

ACROSS: 6 Seaworthiness, **8** Maniac, **9** Ordinary, **10** Rap, **11** Scrape, **12** Herdsmen, **14** Sweeper, **16** Adoring, **20** Frontage, **23** Madame, **24** Lei, **25** Lacrosse, **26** Navajo, **27** Thought-reader. **DOWN: 1** Badinage, **2** Concrete, **3** Atrophy, **4** Kinder, **5** Beings, **6** Search warrant, **7** Sergeant-major, **13** Duo, **15** Pot, **17** Dominoes, **18** Redivide, **19** Celesta, **21** Narrow, **22** Assign.

Week 1

ACROSS: 1 Republican, **6** Warm, **10** Aloha, **11** Statement, **12** Panorama, **13** Later, **15** Triplet, **17** Tagetes, **19** Content, **21** Matinee, **22** Sense, **24** Artistry, **27** Increases, **28** Nadir, **29** List, **30** Impediment. **DOWN: 1** Roam, **2** Probation, **3** Beano, **4** Instant, **5** Adamant, **7** Agent, **8** Mattresses, **9** Red light, **14** Stock-still, **16** Liege men, **18** Tonbridge, **20** Transom, **21** Matisse, **23** Nicks, **25** Sinai, **26** Grit.

NOTES

NOTES

NOTES